LETTER
AND SPIRIT

"This significant book happily trespasses the boundaries that have accidentally accrued in the discipline of theology. It simultaneously concerns itself with the Bible and the liturgy and covenant history and mystagogy and eschatology—in other words, it is a book about connections. It delves into how to connect the believer with the Bible, the Bible with the liturgy, and the liturgy with the economy of God. The name for this theological ligature is 'covenant,' and Hahn shows how God's covenant reaches us even today. In accomplishing this impressive synthesis, he shows himself a comprehensive and accumulative thinker who can place recent scholarship from multiple fields at the service of specialist and layman alike.

"Hahn proposes a living relationship between Scripture and liturgy in order to draw believers into full, active, and conscious participation in salvation history. The way into God's mystery is through the mystical liturgy. In asserting this, Hahn does not lean into the wind of one passing prejudice or another, but rather stands upright on the tradition, saving us from both dead conservatism and errant innovation. His important contribution is to invite us to once again integrate salvation history, sacred text, and Christian ritual so that the Bible's letter will function as spirit in the heart of the liturgical mystery."

—David W. Fagerberg, University of Notre Dame, author of *Theologia Prima: What is Liturgical Theology?*

"With this book Scott Hahn reaffirms a whole new perspective for contemporary biblical scholars. Alongside the motif of the preached word as a fundamental unstated background of the contemporary New Testament scholar he offers the motif of the liturgical act. This new perspective is not a magic key which will transform research in Scripture. But it just might nudge some scholars into looking to the liturgy for new answers to old problems."

—Fr. James Swetnam, S.J., Pontifical Biblical Institute, Rome

"Most Catholics today are likely to think of Mass as something we people do. God's role, except for Communion, is to receive what we do—kindly, we hope. In *Letter and Spirit* Dr. Scott Hahn shines a bright light on what God does at Mass, especially through the proclamation of the word. The proclamation of the word in the Church's liturgy is something far more than reading scriptural texts. As Dr. Hahn writes, 'God's word . . . when it is proclaimed in the liturgy, establishes the kingdom of heaven on earth.' *Letter and Spirit* helps us recover the real significance of the current lectionary and the liturgy of the word in Vatican II's liturgical renewal. What power for individual believers, for the Church, for the world lies within the liturgical proclamation of God's word."

—Bishop Daniel Conlon, Diocese of Steubenville

"Dr. Hahn has again penetrated deeply into the wisdom of Church tradition in this scholarly work dealing with the interrelationship of scripture and liturgy."

—Fr. Michael Scanlan, TOR, Chancellor
Franciscan University of Steubenville

"Experience the life-changing power of God's word in its most natural setting: the community gathered for worship. Readers will profit by this book and be better able to mediate the riches of the Scripture and the liturgy."

—Fr. Francis Martin, Research Fellow
in Catholic Biblical Studies, The Intercultural Forum
of the John Paul II Cultural Center, Washington, D.C.

LETTER AND SPIRIT

From Written Text to Living Word in the Liturgy

SCOTT HAHN

DOUBLEDAY

New York • London • Toronto • Sydney • Auckland

PUBLISHED BY DOUBLEDAY
a division of Random House, Inc.

DOUBLEDAY and the portrayal of an anchor with a dolphin are registered
trademarks of Random House, Inc.

Library of Congress Cataloging-in-Publication Data

Hahn, Scott.
Letter and Spirit : from written text to living Word in the liturgy / Scott
Hahn.— 1st ed.
p. cm.
Includes bibliographical references and index.
(alk. paper)
1. Catholic Church—Liturgy.   2. Bible—Liturgical use.   I. Title.
BX1970.H258 2005
264'.02—dc22   2005045569

Nihil Obstat: Reverend Michael F. Hull, STD, Censor Librorum.
Imprimatur: Most Reverend Robert A. Brucato, Auxiliary Bishop and Vicar
General, Archdiocese of New York.

ISBN 0-385-50933-2

To my seminarians

CONTENTS

FOREWORD

By Jeremy Driscoll, O.S.B.

A WONDROUS THOUGHT: God, the Lord of the Universe, has spoken to us a saving Word! But how can we be sure that it is the Lord's Word we hear? Where do we hear it? In the scriptures, of course. Yes—but how can we know that we are reading these rightly, that what we understand is what they truly mean? There is an answer. The scriptures are heard rightly when they are read in the heart of the church, and this happens at the heart of the liturgy.

Scott Hahn's book *Letter and Spirit* is an extensive exploration of how the scriptures come alive and reach their fullest pitch as they are proclaimed in the liturgical assembly of the believing church. As the author succinctly puts it, scripture is about liturgy and for liturgy. All who study and reflect about scripture will want to learn well—or be reminded of—the basic point of this book: namely, that it was the community at worship that produced the biblical texts and it is in the community at worship that these texts find their fullest sense. This book substantiates this claim and develops its consequences for biblical interpretation. It does so by reviewing the theological terms, exploring the key theological concepts, and discussing the liturgical practices that build up this whole biblical-liturgical world. That said, scripture, of course, emerges also out of the community's lived experience of its covenant with God, and it makes sense of our everyday lives, of our sufferings and joys.

While Dr. Hahn was writing this book, he was reading one I had written, and I too was writing another while reading one of his. I was reading *The Lamb's Supper*; he was reading my *Theology at the Eucharistic Table*. We had the opportunity to speak together several times during this period and found that much of what we wanted to do was converging. His kind invitation to write this introduction came from those exchanges, an invitation that bid me share some of the points where our books touch closely. The book I was writing at the time is called *What Happens at Mass*, and it deals in part with what *Letter and Spirit* deals with at length. While my book covers all the parts of the Mass, Dr. Hahn's concentrates on one essential and indispensable part of it: the proclamation of the Word of God. Understanding this is essential to understanding the rest of the Mass. The eucharistic liturgy is the deepest sense of the proclaimed Word.

In thinking of the structure of the entire eucharistic rite, as I do in *What Happens at Mass*, it is useful to be aware that it embodies a twofold movement: a movement of God toward the world and of the world toward God. This movement in fact unfolds in a trinitarian and ecclesial shape; that is, God the Father comes through his Son to the church for the sake of the world, and the Spirit illumines and vivifies every dimension of this movement. In the other direction, the church, speaking in the name of the whole world, responds in thanksgiving by offering to the Father the very gift she has received: the Son. The Spirit effects the transformation of the church's gifts into the Body and Blood of the Son.

In the liturgy of the Word—it is here that *Letter and Spirit* is concentrated—this twofold movement is enacted by means of speech. God speaks, and we speak back. If we unfold this into its trinitarian and ecclesial shape, we can say that God speaks through his Son in the Holy Spirit to the church; and the church responds. Christ stands exactly in the middle position of these two directions of movement, and thus he is named Mediator. What God says to the world is his Son, Christ. What the world says back to God is also Christ, the Word made flesh, joined to the church. The church also plays the role of mediator here. God speaks to the world in speaking to the church. The church speaks for the world in responding to God. To show that this is the fullest sense and use of scripture is the concern of Dr. Hahn's book.

In our discussions Dr. Hahn and I found ourselves especially excited about the convergence in our thoughts on something I call—having learned the term from the great Italian liturgist Salvatore Marsili—the event character of the proclamation of the Word. The "Word of God" in the liturgy of the Word does not mean the words of the Bible considered merely as words like our words. The Word of God is an event: the event of creation and the event of what God is doing and saying in Israel and finally the event of what God is doing and saying in Jesus. The words of the Bible narrate the event. They are a precious means to us, for they are given by the Holy Spirit. As such, they carry far more than mere human words can carry. They carry the very events of which they speak, and in their formulation is revealed the deepest meaning of the event. In the proclamation of these words, the event proclaimed becomes present. The words in the book are rather like the notes of a musical score. The score is not the music. But the score lets the music sound. When from the score of the biblical book the words are proclaimed in the midst of a believing assembly, the music of God's events sounds forth in the midst of that assembly! What is the basic shape of the music? God speaks to the world, and the world speaks to God. God "says" his Son to the world, and the world "says" itself as Son back to God.

No matter what particular readings occur in a given liturgy, the liturgy of the Word always has about it an event character; that is, the events of the past that are proclaimed become events for the believing community that hears them told. And all the events of the scripture find their center in the one event that is the center of them all: the death and resurrection of Jesus. It is this about which all the scriptures speak. Every proclamation of the Word in the liturgy is an irreducibly new moment. The event of Christ in and through which God once acted to save his people, that same event is delivered here and now to this assembly by means of the biblical score, the gift of the Spirit to the church.

The event of Christ—and of course, all the events of scripture are the event of Christ—becomes the event of the church. The Word proclaimed in liturgy is not some pale reflection or residue of the event proclaimed there. It is the whole reality to which the words bear testimony made present. What was spread out as a series of events through time is now concentrated into the one event of this liturgy. Readers of *Letter and Spirit* will deepen their grasp of all these various dimensions of the biblical words, whose sense expands more and more when proclaimed in the liturgical assembly. I am saying only briefly here what this book spells out at length, justifying these claims historically and theologically.

As the book's arguments advance and the evidence mounts, the reader will gain a stronger and stronger sense of the presence of Christ, the intense presence of Christ, in the proclaimed Word. To speak with the language of some of the chapters' titles, we could say that the covenant—in some sense always the content of the biblical text—is actualized as it is remembered. This actualization is nothing less than a *parousia,* a coming of Christ that already participates in his definitive coming in glory. This is the living sense of tradition—not old ideas from the past that we still for some reason hold on to, but the divine presence that emerges through the written word of scripture in the here and now of the assembly animated by the Spirit. This intense presence of Christ is Apocalypse, that is, a vision that opens into the heavenly liturgies unveiled in the last book of the Bible. Mystagogy is the Church's way of teaching the biblical text such that its words open into this widest heavenly sense, a sense whose future fullness already invades the present of liturgical proclamation.

Mystagogy also shows the way that leads from the liturgy of the Word to the liturgy of the eucharist. *Letter and Spirit* carefully leads the reader into this way. We are brought step by step forward into the divine logic of the eucharistic liturgy, and we can again and again sense the eucharistic liturgy seeping backward into Dr. Hahn's explanations of the biblical word.

This pattern, to borrow a phrase of my own, is what happens at Mass. I have emphasized here that the biblical words ultimately center on the death and resurrection of Christ and the event character of these words when proclaimed. The scriptural words proclaimed in the liturgy become sacrament; that is, the ritual actions and words performed around the community's gifts of bread and wine proclaim in their own way, at an even deeper level, the one and only event of salvation: the Lord's death and resurrection. All other events are gathered into this. And the ritual words and actions proclaim that event as the very event of the community's celebration: *parousia,* Apocalypse, now. The bread and cup are a "communion," as St. Paul says, in the body of Christ, in the blood of Christ (1 Cor 10:16). That is, the bread and cup put the celebrating community into participatory relation with the event of salvation history, an hour that does not pass away. To move "from written text to living Word" is to open the Bible and to receive from it the body and blood of Christ in the heart of the church.

It is above all through the liturgy that Christians come into contact with scripture . . . Christ is then present in his word, because it is he himself who speaks when sacred scripture is read in the Church. Written text thus becomes living word.

PONTIFICAL BIBLICAL COMMISSION,
The Interpretation of the Bible in the Church

INTRODUCTION

FOR READERS WHO know my popular work—some dozen books, including *The Lamb's Supper*—this book will appear to be a departure. For scholars who know my academic work—in *Catholic Biblical Quarterly,* the *Journal of Biblical Literature,* and elsewhere—this book will appear to be a departure. *Letter and Spirit* is neither a work of technical exegesis, nor a popular or remedial treatment of biblical and doctrinal themes.

Letter and Spirit is the first book I have written for both audiences. I wrote it for those whose interest has been piqued by my popular books and are ready to go deeper in their study. But I wrote it especially for my colleagues and my students, with whom I have been exploring, for almost three decades, the relationship between scripture and liturgy. We all seem to agree that such a study is overdue. For years I waited for someone to write it. I thank my editors at Doubleday for urging me to stop waiting and start writing. Anything that's worth doing is worth doing as well as I can do it.

How well I have done, this time, I leave it to my readers to judge.

Catholics have now entered the second century of the modern biblical and liturgical movements, if we take as our (somewhat arbitrary) starting point the institutional reforms of Pope Pius X. Those initial efforts were seeds that came to flower in the Second Vatican Council (1962–65). It is tremendously significant that the council produced three dogmatic constitutions, and that they were on three interrelated realities: liturgy, divine revelation, and the church. We might even call them aspects of the same reality, so closely are they related. It is their interrelationship that I will address in the pages of this book.

Over the last generation, liturgical reform has been something of a spectator sport, with the players, ex-players, and journalists providing play-by-play and color commentary in the media. Most observers say that the most seismic change came with Pope Paul VI's promulgation of the new order of the Mass in 1970—when, suddenly, the priest was facing the people rather than the tabernacle, the liturgy was recited in the vernacular language rather than Latin, and so on. And those were momentous changes.

I believe, however, that the most significant change came about in 1969, with the introduction of the revised lectionary.[1] The media missed this one because there was so little controversy. Almost everyone agreed that the finished product was a remarkable achievement. And there can be no doubt that it was a major development in the life of the church. The lectionary was designed specifically for the purpose of highlighting the essential relationship between scripture and liturgy.[2] The old lectionary had covered a one-year cycle; the new book covered three years. The old lectionary's Sunday readings had been chosen almost exclusively from the gospels and epistles; the new lectionary employed most of the content of most of the books of the Bible, both the Old and New Testaments. In the old lectionary, the Sunday gospels had not been selected in any representative or proportionate way; there were, I believe, only four readings from Mark in a year, and the parable of the prodigal son was not read at all.[3]

The three-year lectionary was an ecumenical event. Within a year, the Presbyterian churches imitated it, and Anglican and Lutheran bodies soon adopted it as well. This, in itself, is a remarkable development. A common lectionary establishes a common collective memory, a common "calendrical narrative,"[4] and so a firmer common ground for ecumenical dialogue.[5]

At the same time as these ecclesiastical developments came the rise, in academia, of "canonical criticism," best exemplified in the work of Brevard Childs of Yale University. The Pontifical Biblical Commission described this movement with remarkable clarity:

> The "canonical" approach . . . proceeds from the perception that the historical-critical method experiences at times considerable difficulty in arriving, in its conclusions, at a truly theological level. It aims to carry out the theological task of interpretation more successfully by beginning from within an

explicit framework of faith: the Bible as a whole. To achieve this, it interprets each biblical text in the light of the canon of Scriptures, that is to say, of the Bible as received as the norm of faith by a community of believers. It seeks to situate each text within the single plan of God.[6]

Canonical criticism facilitated the study of scripture's individual books within the context of the entire Book. Perceptive scholars took this notion a step further and considered the Bible as not just a literary unity, but also a liturgical unity. Indeed it is the liturgy that provides a "focused interpretation"[7] of the canon for the entire People of God. I am indebted to these scholars, and I hope, with this book, to make their work more widely known. Thus I hope I will be forgiven my rather extensive use of quotation.

I wish, however, to situate my discussion in something other than the contemporary ecumenical debate about the canonical approach to scripture. I want to draw deeply from the Catholic tradition: the scriptures and liturgies, the fathers, the schoolmen, the councils and popes—and the great theologians. Academic readers will recognize my dependence on certain works: M. J. Scheeben's *The Mysteries of Christianity*; Jean Danielou's *The Bible and the Liturgy*; Henri de Lubac's *Medieval Exegesis*; Augustin Cardinal Bea's *The Word of God and Mankind*; Cyprian Vagaggini's *Theological Dimensions of the Liturgy*; Jean Corbon's *The Wellspring of Worship*; Yves Congar's *The Meaning of Tradition*; Enrico Mazza's *Mystagogy*; and Joseph Ratzinger's *The Spirit of the Liturgy*.

I am convinced that we have not yet begun to appreciate

the great changes that have taken place in the church, especially with regard to the revision of the lectionary. We have only begun to assimilate the change. This book, *Letter and Spirit,* is my personal beginning, my initial effort to understand this great historical moment in the history of so many convergent movements: liturgical, biblical, patristic, and ecumenical.

It is a beginning on paper. My students and my seminarians will recognize many of the ideas that follow. They have challenged me, through almost twenty-five years of teaching, to say what I mean with ever-increasing clarity. They have been exacting critics and tireless seekers. For that I am very grateful, and to them I dedicate this book, especially the seminarians, past, present, and future.

CHAPTER 1

OUR NEARNESS
TO THE ANCIENTS

EW STORIES IN Christian antiquity circulated as widely and as rapidly as Athanasius' telling of the life of Anthony, the fourth-century hermit of the Egyptian desert. Within a generation of Anthony's death, Augustine tells us,[1] the book had motivated countless Christians to take up the contemplative life in seclusion. The drama in Athanasius' narrative turned on a single moment in Anthony's youth.

> *Not six months after the death of his parents, he went according to custom to the Lord's house . . . He entered the church, and it happened the Gospel was being read, and he heard the Lord saying to the rich man, "If you would be perfect, go, sell what you possess and give to the poor, and you will have treasure in heaven" [Mt 19:21]. Anthony, . . . as if the passage had been read on his account, went out immediately from the church, and gave the possessions of his forefathers to the villagers . . . All the rest that was movable he sold, and having got together much money he gave it to the poor, reserving a little, however, for his sister's sake . . . And again he went into the church, and he heard the Lord*

say in the Gospel, "do not be anxious about your life" [Mt 6:25]. He could stay no longer, but went out and gave those things also to the poor . . . he henceforth devoted himself outside his house to discipline.[2]

It is a rich passage for those who wish to understand the history of biblical interpretation. Athanasius' *Life of Anthony* made a profound impression on the greatest exegetes of the next generations: Augustine, Jerome, Rufinus, Evagrius. And the author himself, Athanasius, played a crucial role in the history of the formation of the New Testament canon.

For our purposes, though, the passage is important not so much because of its effects or its author, but because of the window it opens upon biblical interpretation in an early Christian community.

What we encounter in this episode is not merely evidence of a received text—two stories from Matthew's gospel—but also the very process of reception. Anthony's turning point came at the mid-third century, when the canon had not yet reached a final and universal form.

Athanasius shows us, here as elsewhere, that the ordinary place of biblical interpretation was the church, and the ordinary time was the liturgy. In the ancient world, the church's liturgy—its public, ritual worship—was the natural and supernatural habitat of the church's scriptures.

This was true not only of the Christian *ekklesia* (church), but also of the *qahal* (assembly) of ancient Israel, which proclaimed and chanted the scriptures in its liturgies of synagogue, temple, and home. Biblical religion was liturgical religion, and its sacred texts were primarily liturgical texts. This is what makes the witness of the church fathers so valuable for biblical studies. Christopher Hall speaks of the fathers' "hermeneutical proximity"—their interpretive nearness—to the biblical world. The overwhelming witness of the fathers and the rabbis is not an accumulation of the conclusions of scientific exegesis, but rather a great mass of liturgical sermons, catechetical lectures, and rubrics for worship. Even the "passing on" of the texts and doctrines—for Christians the *traditio* and *redditio*—was, then as now, a liturgical action. The Christian fathers received the texts, prayed the texts, proclaimed the texts, venerated the texts, and passed on the texts in ways that were similar to, and continuous with, those of their apostolic and Jewish ancestors.

For both Jews and Christians, the scriptural texts, though historical in character, were not merely records of past events. Reading them in public was more than just the preservation of a national saga. The scriptures were intended to sweep the worshiper into their action—"as if the passage had been read on his account." More than two centuries after Jesus spoke his words to the rich young man and to the crowd, Anthony (and his biographer) assumed that the words were addressed directly to himself. The historical words were *actualized* again in the life of a contemporary listener, a contemporary worshiper. And Anthony's own participation in salvation history was itself history-making for future generations.

Biblical scholarship of the last century and a half has profited immeasurably from the wider cultural current of historical consciousness—that is, the growing awareness of the conditioning influence of historical and cultural circumstances. Perhaps more than any other field, biblical exegesis has tested the limits of the historical-critical method. If we are more aware today of the common liturgical ground of Israel's *qahal* and Christianity's *ekklesia*, it is because of these movements in scholarship, aided by important discoveries in other fields, not least in archeology and textual and documentary analysis.

In our diligent pursuit of the Bible's elusive *Sitz im Leben* (its original life-setting), we find ourselves, surprisingly, in a familiar place: in the ritual public worship of the congregation. If we can hope for any insight into our proto-Christian and Israelite forebears, it is because we, like the fathers Anthony and Athanasius, share something in common with the ancients. Cardinal Joseph Ratzinger has warned against a too-eager appropriation of the fathers: "to return to the classical work and to omit what we have learned over the last two hundred years is not a possibility."[3] But it is arguably the best critical scholarship that has led us again to that original setting. "As to the origin of the Scriptures," wrote scholar Geoffrey Wainwright, "much of their material . . . has been judged by contemporary scholarship to have had its *Sitz im Leben* in the worship of the believing community."[4]

Liturgy is the very place of our interpretive nearness to the ancients. In our present is our beginning.

When I speak of liturgy, I mean the ritual public worship of God's covenant people. I speak primarily of the eucharistic liturgy, but not only that; for all the sacramental liturgies, as well as the liturgy of the hours, find their origin and source in the scriptures—and are similarly saturated with biblical texts. And all the church's liturgies share with the scriptures a common end: *Deo omnis gloria*—all the glory to God.

In the course of this book, I want to explore the liturgical content of the Bible and the liturgical context in which the scriptures were first produced, canonized, and proclaimed. I hope to demonstrate the living relationship between scripture and liturgy, and how this relationship enables both, together, to draw believers, as active participants, into the divine drama of salvation history.

CHAPTER 2

DEFINING TERMS

NOWHERE IS THE relationship between Bible and
liturgy presented so vividly and succinctly as in
the Bible itself, specifically in Luke's account of
the conversation on the road to Emmaus (Lk 24:13–25).

It is the Sunday after Jesus' crucifixion. Two disciples
make their way along the road from Jerusalem when they
are joined by a third man. It is Jesus, Luke tells us, but the
disciples "are kept from recognizing him." Jesus questions
them and draws out their dismal account of the previous Fri-
day's events. They conclude by expressing their frustrated
hopes: "But we had hoped that he was the one to redeem Israel."

Jesus (still incognito to the two) weighs in immediately
with his judgment, faulting them for their lack of faith,
which he describes in terms of a failure to receive the scriptures properly: "O foolish men, and slow of heart to believe
all that the prophets have spoken!" (v. 25). He follows, logically, by correcting their interpretation, replacing it with a
thoroughgoing exegesis of his own. Significantly, Luke dis-
closes not the content of Jesus' interpretation, but rather his
method: "beginning with Moses and all the prophets, he in-

terpreted to them in all the scriptures the things concerning himself."

Later, the disciples will reflect on their hearing and say, "Did not our hearts burn within us while he talked to us on the road, while he opened to us the scriptures?" For the moment, however, their understanding is incomplete, and they ask the stranger to remain with them when they stop for the night's lodging. It is then that the passage reaches its narrative climax: "When he was at table with them, he took the bread and blessed, and broke it, and gave it to them. And their eyes were opened and they recognized him; and he vanished out of their sight."

Shortly thereafter, when they encounter the apostles, they tell the story of "what had happened on the road, and how he was known to them in the breaking of the bread."

Volumes of biblical and liturgical theology have been written interpreting only this passage. Here, I would like merely to draw out three characteristics of Jesus' method, encapsulated in three technical terms: *economy, typology,* and *mystagogy.*

There is a certain novelty to these terms, though none is new. Two appear prominently in the New Testament, and all three stand out as hallmarks of early Christian exegesis. Yet, in the first half of the twentieth century, they received scant attention in the theological manuals and almost no attention from scholars. All three have since reentered the vocabulary. Their recovery is attributable at least in part to three theological movements: the biblical, the liturgical, and the patristic.

Economy, typology, mystagogy: Since these terms are key to the argument of the rest of the book, and their recovery has been recent and intermittent, it will be good to spend some time discussing them now, in an integrated way, using the Emmaus passage of Luke's gospel as a touchstone.

Economy

Jesus' exposition on the road to Emmaus included "all the scriptures" "beginning with Moses and all the prophets." Implicit in this is a unity of purpose throughout the many diverse sacred books of the Jews. Jesus discerned there an orderly plan, unfolding throughout history and expressed in the inspired record, a plan that would culminate in his own saving work.

This notion of an overarching plan in creation and salvation history is hardly peculiar to the Emmaus episode. It is everywhere in Hebrew and Christian thought; and it finds its summary statement in Ephesians 1:9, which describes "the plan of the mystery hidden for ages in God who created all things." The Greek word translated here as "plan" is *oikonomia* (Latin, *dispensatio*). Etymologically, it derives from *oikos* and *nomos, household* and *law.* The *oikonomia,* the divine economy, is the principle governing all creation as well as all the events of salvation history. It is the law of God's cosmic "household."

The domestic association is richly suggestive. For Paul, history revealed God's fatherly plan for humankind. Later, both the church fathers and their rabbinic contemporaries spoke of the scriptures in terms of "divine accommodation"—God stooping down to communicate with his children on their level, or lifting them up to see from a divine perspective. In the third century, Origen wrote of this as a manifestation of God's fatherhood: "whenever the divine plan *[oikonomia]* involves human affairs, God takes on human intelligence, manners, and language, just as when we talk to a child of two we talk baby-talk."[1] Origen was surely building here upon the Septuagint, which renders Deuteronomy 1:31: "The Lord your God took on your manners as a man would take on the manners of his son."

A modern rabbi and scholar, Stephen D. Benin, traced the patterns of divine accommodation in Jewish and Christian thought and finds a consistent paternal purpose in God's condescension and elevation. Benin concluded: "God uses history pedagogically."[2] He teaches through the events that correspond to his eternal plan.

This Pauline term *oikonomia* was to dominate patristic theology and exegesis. Indeed, *oikonomia* is sometimes translated into English simply as "theology," though that is an imprecision. In the writings of the Greek fathers, the word *theologia* refers specifically to doctrine and contemplation of the Trinity. *Oikonomia* refers more broadly to God's dealings with creation.[3] Jean Corbon pointed out, further, that *oikonomia* means "more than simply the 'history of salvation'; it is the dispensation, or wise arrangement by stages, whereby the mystery that is Christ is brought to fulfillment."[4]

Theology and economy are, of course, related terms, and the modern academy includes both activities within the field of theology. The *Catechism of the Catholic Church* (n. 236) distinguishes the terms even as it demonstrates their relationship:

> *The Fathers of the Church distinguish between theology* (theologia) *and economy* (oikonomia). *"Theology" refers to the mystery of God's inmost life within the Blessed Trinity and "economy" to all the works by which God reveals himself and communicates his life. Through the* oikonomia *the* theologia *is revealed to us; but conversely, the* theologia *illuminates the whole* oikonomia. *God's works reveal who he is in himself; the mystery of his inmost being enlightens our understanding of all his works.*

Indeed, the *Catechism*'s editor, Cardinal Christoph Schonborn, identified the *oikonomia* as the *"leitmotiv* running through the whole of the new *Catechism . . .* It is certain that the theme of the *divine economy* is woven through all four parts" [italics in original].[5]

Schonborn goes on to sketch the trinitarian shape of the economy: "The whole of the divine economy has no other source or purpose than this infinitely blissful [trinitarian] life: the economy is therefore expressed in accordance with the great moments of the communication of this life: the word of creation and divine governance (Providence), the work of redemption through Jesus Christ and the work of sanctification in the Holy Spirit through the Church. . . . in the age of the Church, it becomes the sacramental economy."[6] Corbon anticipated this conclusion: "From Pentecost on, the economy has become liturgy because we are in the stage of response and of the synergy . . . of Spirit and Church."[7]

What Christ revealed at Emmaus, then, was nothing less than the plan, the dramatic plot, the story line for all of history before him and after him. By unveiling the "things concerning him" "in all the scriptures," he made possible the work of exegesis and of biblical theology. His interpretation of the entirety of the Hebrew scriptures functioned like an act of canonization, precluding all future attempts (such as Marcion's) to excise the "Old Testament" as obsolete. Christ himself made Israel's scriptures canonical as he made them one with his new covenant.

Moreover, he modeled what would become biblical religion's defining action during the age of the church, the time of the sacramental economy. He revealed himself conclusively "in the breaking of the bread." The "breaking of the bread" is Luke's preferred term for the eucharist; and in the Lukan Acts of the Apostles, the eucharistic "breaking of the bread" is the preeminent sign of the church (see Acts 2:42, 46; 20:7, 11; 27:35).

Typology

Our attention to the divine economy leads us logically to a typological reading of scripture. The *Catechism of the Catholic Church* puts it simply: "typology . . . discerns in God's works of the Old Covenant prefigurations of what he accomplished in the fullness of time" (n. 128).

Typology is implicit in the twofold literary structure of the Bible. The economy governs a single story, but it is composed of two parts: the Old Testament and the New. Typology is the literal sense in which the New Testament reads the Old. Indeed, typology refers precisely to those things that Christ revealed in his exegesis on the road to Emmaus—"the things concerning him" "in all the scriptures." The other New Testament writers follow his example in applying "all the scriptures" to their doctrine on the church and Christian moral, ascetical, and sacramental life. It is not merely, or even primarily, a correspondence of prediction and fulfillment. It is, rather, a pattern of analogy. What began in the Old Testament is fulfilled partially even within the Old Testament, but definitively in the New, in a way that is both transformative and restorative.

The word "typology" derives from the use of the Greek word *typos* in several New Testament passages. In one, Paul tells us that "Adam . . . was a type of the one who was to come" (Rom 5:14). We find another in 1 Peter, which tells of the family of Noah being "saved through water"; baptism, we are told, "corresponds to this" (1 Pt 3:21). In this latter passage, the Greek says, literally, that baptism is an *antitypon,* or antitype, of the flood. As a "type" is a prefiguring sign, an "antitype" is the thing signified.

The term *typos* predates Christian usage. Its literal meaning is the impression of a seal upon wax, or of a die upon a coin. All these impressions (types) correspond to far greater realities (antitypes). The type represents the emperor whose image appears on the coin, or the judge who notarized the document. Philosophers had long applied the terms metaphorically in discussions of literary works, to discuss, for example, a foreshadowing event in a drama.

Typology, then, would be the study of types, or wisdom regarding types; and the method is characteristic of the Old Testament as well as the New. Many scholars have noted that the Book of Exodus, at many points, seems to depict the events of Israel's exodus as a reprise of the creation stories of Genesis. The newborn Moses, for example, was set afloat (Ex 2:3) in a vessel identified with the same Hebrew word used to describe the "ark" of Noah (Gen 6:14). From the midst of the Red Sea, Israel emerged as a new nation (Ex 14:26–29), just as in Genesis the world emerged from the deep, dark primeval waters (Gen 1:1–2). The making of the priestly vestments and the building of the tabernacle again recall the creation narrative. In both, the work is done in seven stages, each punctuated with the words "as the Lord commanded Moses." Moses, like God, beholds his handiwork, and blesses it (Ex 39:43). As God "finished his work," so Moses "finished the work" (Gen 2:1–2; Ex 40:34). And as God rested on the seventh day after completing his work and blessed and hallowed the day, when Moses is finished with his work, the divine presence of God fills the tabernacle (Ex 40:34).

The prophets, in turn, read the Torah typologically, and they saw its historical events as harbingers of events in their own day and in the more distant future. Henri de Lubac, drawing from the work of Jean Danielou, spoke of a "prehistory" of typological exegesis found in the Old Testament: "the prophets themselves give notice of 'a second Exodus, of which the first was a mere figurative symbol' . . . and for Ezekiel the description of the first paradise is projected onto his vision of the Last Jerusalem."[8] We can discern, for example, in Isaiah, Jeremiah, and Ezekiel the constant interpretation of redemptive events, present and future, in terms that evoke a new creation (Is 4:5, 65:17, 66:22; Jer 31:35–36; Ezek 36:8–11), new exodus (Is 51:9–11; Jer 16:14–15; Ezek 29:3–5), and new kingdom (Is 9:2–7; Jer 23:5–6; Ezek 34:23–24).[9] Creation, exodus, and the establishment of the kingdom are arguably the three most significant divine acts in history, as far as the biblical writers are concerned. Thus, creation, exodus, and kingdom appear as the three "mountain peaks" of typology throughout the major and minor prophets and, later, throughout the New Testament.

Typology has always been integral to biblical revelation, and this is nowhere evident as in the prophets. Indeed, Danielou spoke of "the organic relation between typology and prophecy," and he defined prophecy as "the typological interpretation of history."[10]

Typology was vital to pagan literature as well, but it served a fundamentally different purpose. Biblical typology, unlike that of the Greek philosophers, was not mere literary analysis. It had a certain, *and primarily,* historical significance. Judaeo-Christian typological interpretation assumes, and even depends upon, the historicity of the prefiguring events as well as the realities that are their fulfillment. Danielou summarized well the teaching of Augustine and Aquinas when he said that typology is not merely "a meaning of words," but "a meaning of things"—not merely "a sense of scripture," but "a sense of history."[11]

Typological exegesis, then, presumes the idea of the divine economy. History unfolds, like all creation, according to a single divine plan. Augustine explained that ordinary human writers use words to signify things; but God uses even created *things* to signify things. So not only are the *words* of scripture signs of things that happened in history, but the *very events of sacred history* were fashioned by God as material signs—temporal events and realities that disclose eternal truths. "The process by which the events correspond can be called typology."[12]

This way of understanding history and creation, so habitual to the prophets and the rabbis, was the patrimony inherited by the first generation of Christians. Thus, the practice of typology affects every page of the New Testament. The evangelists and apostolic authors do not hesitate to apply the words of the Hebrew prophets to events in the life of Christ: from his virginal conception to his humiliating death. They are as eager also to use Old Testament allusions to draw parallels between Christ and the ancestral heroes. He appears often as a new Adam, a new Moses, and the Son of David, thus recapitulating the three "mountain peaks" (creation, exodus, and kingdom) that we observed in the typology of the prophets. "The New Testament . . . did not invent typology, but simply showed that it was fulfilled in the person of Jesus of Nazareth."[13]

Moreover, since typology depends upon scripture's literal-historical sense, the New Testament's exegesis of the Old depends upon the enduring integrity of the Hebrew scriptures. In the words of Hugh of St. Victor: "History is the foundation." Danielou rightly observed: "The typological interpretation of events does not in any way tend to ignore or mask their individual existence and value, but affords a frame of reference for intelligible coordination."[14]

Apparently, typology provided Jesus with the "frame of reference" in his unrecorded discourse on the road to Emmaus. What else but a typological exegesis could describe "the things concerning him" "in all the scriptures"—that is, in the Old Testament?

Typology has had its share of detractors, both ancient and modern. But the method has always had its defenders, even among historical critics. Gerhard von Rad defended typology on anthropological grounds: "typological thinking is an elementary function of all human thought and interpretation."[15] Christopher Wright spoke, similarly, of typology as "a normal and common way of knowing and understanding things . . . Any teacher knows that in introducing new ideas or skills, you have to work by analogy or correspondence from what is already known and familiar—either past events, or experience, or pre-understandings."[16] We should, then, expect any human authors to employ typological techniques. And, since "all scripture is inspired by God" (2 Tim 3:16), we may further discern, in the Bible, a *divine pedagogy* at work in both the writings and in the actual events of salvation history.

Typological exegesis, then, describes the pattern of promise and fulfillment in salvation history, identifying the key events, persons, and institutions. Typology depends upon the unity of the whole Bible and upon the salvific intent of God from all eternity. Typology assumes, in the words of Augustine, that the New Testament is concealed in the Old, and the Old is revealed in the New—conclusively revealed in Jesus Christ, who himself "opens . . . the scriptures" to disciples, who come to know him, then, "in the breaking of the bread."

Mystagogy

We find in the disciples' journey from Jerusalem to Emmaus a movement toward illumination. It is an illumination we might categorize as "mystagogy." Literally, "mystagogy" (from the Greek *mystagogia)* means a "doctrine of the mysteries" or "doctrine of the sacraments." More precisely, it is typology applied to the sacraments. In the words of Danielou: "the sacraments carry on in our midst the *mirabilia,* the great works of God in the Old Testament and the New."[17]

Mystagogy is, according to Mazza, "the oral or written explanation of the mystery hidden in the scriptures and celebrated in the liturgy."[18] To Robert Taft it is a logical extension of biblical interpretation: "All healthy liturgical interpretation depends on a ritual symbolism determined not arbitrarily, but by the testimony of tradition rooted in the Bible. Like the scriptures, the rites of the Church await an exegesis and a hermeneutic and a homiletic to expound, interpret, and apply their multiple levels of meaning in each age. *Mystagogy is to liturgy what exegesis is to scripture* [emphasis mine]. It is no wonder, then, that the commentators on the liturgy used a method inherited from the older tradition of biblical exegesis."[19] That tradition is evident in the Bible itself.

As evening fell upon the first Easter Sunday, the disciples' unknown companion led them to an understanding of the divine economy and its typological pattern, now newly fulfilled.

Part of the process was didactic. Christ guided the disciples by interpreting "all the scriptures" for them. But the definitive part was pure grace. At the decisive moment, when the disciples owned the knowledge of Christ as the summit of the divine economy and the fulfillment of the types, the evangelist describes the process with a passive verb form: "he was known to them [or "was made known to them"] in the breaking of the bread." It is Jesus' eucharistic action that brought about the disciples' recognition.

What Paul calls "the plan of the mystery hidden for ages" was now revealed to the disciples, though not in a way they could see with their eyes. For, immediately, Jesus "vanished out of their sight." The mysteries of Christ's life—culminating in his passion, death, and resurrection—had fulfilled the typological signs of the Old Testament. This fulfillment, however, did not lead disciples immediately into the beatific vision. It led them, rather, to a reprise of Jesus' "new covenant" meal. On the night he was betrayed, Jesus "took bread, . . . broke it and gave it" to his apostles, saying, "This is my body which is given for you. Do this in remembrance of me" (Lk 22:19).

His physical body they did not recognize; but, after he had prepared them by his typological interpretation of the scriptures, he "was known to them"—by faith, not by sight—in the breaking of the bread.

This is mystagogy. Having been instructed in the pattern of the divine economy, the disciples could see what Cardinal Schonborn described above: "in the age of the Church, it becomes the sacramental economy." Augustine divided salvation history in a similar way: "Before the coming of Christ, the flesh and blood of this sacrifice were foreshadowed in the animals slain; in the passion of Christ the types were fulfilled by the true sacrifice; after the ascension of Christ, this sacrifice is commemorated in the sacrament."[20]

Christ's life has fulfilled the types in a sacrifice that was "once for all" (Heb 9:26). But the mysteries of his life—all that was hidden in his life—are now extended in time through the church's sacraments. After his resurrection, the ordinary way the disciples come to know the mysteries of his life is through the breaking of the bread. This is evident immediately at Emmaus, but borne out also through the Acts of the Apostles and the Pauline corpus. Chapters 5, 10, and 11 of the First Letter to the Corinthians are explicitly mystagogical, describing the eucharistic rite, but also tracing their antecedents in the events and rites of the Old Testament. Paul presents a similar mystagogy of baptism in his letters to the Romans (6), Galatians (3), and, again, 1 Corinthians (6:11 and 10). For Paul, the process of covenant fulfillment by Christ is not terminated but continued in the sacraments.[21]

The *Catechism of the Catholic Church* puts it well: "The mysteries of Christ's life are the foundations of what he would henceforth dispense in the sacraments, through the ministers of his Church" (CCC, n. 1115). The *Catechism* concludes with a quotation from Leo the Great: "what was visible in our Savior has passed over into his mysteries."

The sacraments and the mysteries—the fathers used the terms somewhat interchangeably, for they describe the same phenomena. But it is good for us to make a distinction. The term "sacrament" emphasizes the visible signs in the church's rites, while "mystery" emphasizes the hidden reality. "Sacrament" has always been the preferred term of the Christian West (with Leo, perhaps, being the great exception), while "mystery" has dominated in the East.

Mystagogy, according to the *Catechism,* is a process that moves us "from the visible to the invisible, from the sign to the thing signified, from the 'sacraments' to the 'mysteries' " (n. 1075). It is a process that involves both human and divine initiatives, both human dispositions and divine grace. Following Jesus' model in Luke 24, it involves both didactic instruction and the experience of liturgy.

What was visible in Christ "has passed over into his mysteries." In the sacraments, he is made known to his disciples, but it is more than a knowledge of doctrine, more than a wisdom about the world. When Christ is "made known . . .

in the breaking of the bread," what is happening is something far more profound than mere learning. It surpasses the mere conversation of wayfarers, no matter how exalted that may be—and it is difficult to imagine conversation more exalted than what must have passed among the travelers on the road to Emmaus.

The New Testament refers to the encounter, in the breaking of the bread, as a *koinonia,* a communion. That is the term used in Acts (2:42) to describe the church's eucharistic fellowship. Paul uses the same word, twice, to describe the Christian's reception of the eucharistic body and blood of Christ (1 Cor 10:16).

The events of Christ's life pass over into the mysteries, where they are continued in the lives of believers. The Christian at liturgy receives a "participation in the blood of Christ," "a participation in the body of Christ," a share in his suffering, death, and resurrection. "The Liturgy consists of this participation of the members of Christ's mystical body in the mysteries which Christ, their Head, originally fulfilled."[22] "Do you not know," Paul writes, "that all of us who have been baptized into Christ Jesus were baptized into his death?" (Rom 6:3).

This is why every eucharistic liturgy conforms to the pattern established at Emmaus: the opening of the scriptures followed by the breaking of the bread, the liturgy of the word followed by the liturgy of the eucharist. The Mass, then, is the place par excellence of the scriptures' faithful reception. It is the place where, by grace and by habit, the scriptures are rendered most intelligible to the disciples and most potent to transform human lives. The breaking of the bread, of itself, is mystagogical, now as it was at Emmaus. Christ is present, and he is made known, even though the disciples cannot see him.

The primary mystagogy of the liturgy, then, belongs to Christ, who is substantially present in the breaking of the bread. Nevertheless, his real presence does not present a free pass to preachers. Liturgical sermons should also be mystagogical—unveiling the hidden mysteries of the divine economy, its typology, and the sacramental economy. Those who preach must follow the example of Christ on the road, as his interpretation set fire to the disciples' hearts. Jeremy Driscoll writes: "All the texts must be brought to the event that encompasses them: the Lord's death and resurrection. . . . [T]hrough the eucharist about to be celebrated, we have communion in the very same death and resurrection."[23]

Most people encounter the word "mystagogy" through their study of patristics. There is, among the writings of the fathers, a certain genre called the "mystagogical homilies" or "mystagogical catecheses." The best-known surviving examples are those of Cyril of Jerusalem, Ambrose of Milan, Theodore of Mopsuestia, John Chrysostom, Augustine, (Pseudo-)Dionysius, and Maximus the Confessor. The ancient church—even as late as the sixth century—tried, ordinarily, to observe a certain reticence regarding the sacraments. The fathers preached and wrote little about specific details of the rites. When they made mention of the liturgy, they often did so in veiled, highly allusive and symbolic language. Later generations referred to this tendency as the *disciplina arcana,* the discipline of the secret. The silence was broken, customarily, only with the Easter homilies that explained the "mysteries" the new Christians had experienced for the first time. Such "mystagogical" homilies were didactic, richly scriptural, but they presupposed the experience of the paschal sacraments of baptism, penance, eucharist, and chrismation.

The mystagogical homily opened the newly baptized Christian's eyes to the sacramental economy in which he lived and moved and had his being. Following the New Testament model, the mystagogical preacher (almost always the local bishop) demonstrated the significance of the biblical types and the sacramental antitypes. These "eye-opening" homilies prepared the new Christian for a lifetime of continued mystagogy, a gradual deepening in knowledge of the mysteries of Jesus Christ and his church. What began with the "breaking of the bread" need never end.

In Luke's account of Christ's teaching on the road to Emmaus, we find three principles that will be indispensable to our further examination of the relationship between scripture and liturgy: economy, typology, mystagogy. John Breck has examined these in a profound way in his exegesis of the Emmaus story, and has shown their application to liturgy today:

Nevertheless, however enriching the Gospel reading may be, however eloquent the sermon, revelation of the divine Word remains incomplete before celebration of the eucharistic mystery. As in the experience of the disciples at Emmaus, the gathered community only "perceives" the full revelation, it only opens its eyes to a true understanding and acceptance of the divine economy, through a personal and intimate communion in the divine gifts of Christ's Body and Blood. The Liturgy of the Word thus comes to fulfillment in and through the Liturgy of the Eucharist, the Sacrament of sacraments that alone transforms the Word from a message about Jesus into a true participation in His divine life.[24]

Economy, typology, mystagogy: Equipped with these, we now begin our journey from Emmaus to the very ends of the canonical scriptures.

CHAPTER 3

THE UNITIES OF SCRIPTURE
AND LITURGY

A T EMMAUS, THE disciples witnessed the summary of a truth that had long been established in biblical religion: the unity of scripture and liturgy. From the beginning, the two have been united indissolubly. Scripture is for liturgy, and scripture is about liturgy. The liturgy, likewise, proclaims the scriptures even as it interprets and actualizes them. The unity of scripture and liturgy may be described as both material and formal.

It is *material* in that the content of scripture is, to a great extent, concerned with the liturgy, and the content of the liturgy is drawn from scripture. Liturgy figures most prominently in salvation history's key moments—creation, the flood, the call of Abram, the exodus, and the founding of the kingdom of David. Scripture, for its part, figures most prominently in every aspect of the liturgy, in both the ritual words and ritual actions. This is most evident in the liturgy of the word, but also in the institution narrative and in many of the standard prayers. Scripture is, in this important sense, *about* liturgy, just as liturgy is *about* scripture.

Their relationship is *formal* in that scripture took its final form—it was canonized—for the sake of liturgy, and the canon itself derived from liturgical tradition. James A. Sanders made this observation of canonical study: "That which is canon comes to us from ancient communities of faith, not just from individuals. . . . [T]he whole of the Bible, the sum as well as all its parts, comes to us out of the liturgical and instructional life of early believing communities."[1]

There is ample evidence for this in the scriptures themselves—e.g., in the giving of the law at Sinai, the ratification of the law at Schechem, the foundation of the temple by David and Solomon, the religious reform under Josiah, and the restoration under Ezra. Biblical religion has always required the proclamation of God's word within the assembly. In the old covenant, that proclamation was public, communal, and liturgical. It remained so with the new covenant of Jesus Christ. For both Jews and Christians, the scriptural texts, though historical in character, are not merely records of past events. The scriptures are intended to sweep the worshiper into their action. Liturgy is the privileged place of this "actualization" of God's word, because the liturgy is itself formed from the scriptures and by the scriptures. Scripture is, in this sense, *for* liturgy.

All of scripture is intrinsically liturgical. Liturgy is like a golden thread that runs through the many pearls of salvation history and holds them together. Remember that the *oikonomia,* the divine economy, refers to all the acts by which God reveals himself and communicates his life. In the Old Testament, these acts often appear as liturgical acts—even when they take place in the midst of battles, family disputes, and the ordinary administration of a nation-state. The divine drama turns on ritual acts of worship, blessing, cursing, oath-swearing, fasting, penance, and, most significantly, sacrifice. In the New Testament, we discover that the liturgies of the Old Testament found typological fulfillment in the sacrifice of Christ. The New Testament reveals as well that Christ's unique sacrifice extends through time in the sacramental liturgy of the church.

The bonds of scripture and liturgy—both formal and material—invite closer examination.

The Material Relationship— The Bible Is About Liturgy

The scholar Eugene Maly described the Old Testament as the historical record of "Israel—God's liturgical people."[2] Maly characterized Israel as "a liturgical people of God marching processionally through the desert"—and indeed through history—"hierarchically grouped behind their Lord, and solemnizing their deliverance from every crisis by an appropriate cultic celebration."[3] Gordon Wenham, in his commentary on Numbers, noted that "more than half of the Pentateuch, always considered the most authoritative section of the Old Testament, consists of ritual regulations, instructions about building the tabernacle, laws on sacrifice and festivals and so on."[4]

Scripture presents this liturgical pattern as beginning with creation. Both ancient rabbis and modern scholars have noted the preponderance of cultic language and imagery in the two creation stories of the Book of Genesis. Klaus Westermann called the first creation account (Gen 1:1–2:4) "a heavenly liturgy."[5] The cosmos itself seems to follow a liturgical calendar. God created the world in six "days" for the sake of the seventh, the sabbath, which he made holy (Gen 2:3). Thus, the first pages of the canonical scriptures set a sabbatical rhythm for all subsequent history. This divine model established the order for humanity: work was ordered to worship, labor to liturgy. Man subdued the earth in order to consecrate its fruits to God. From the beginning, then, God made time holy, and creation itself became a cosmic temple with Adam as its high priest.

Liturgy remains a dominant theme in all the subsequent stages of salvation history. Immediately after the accounts of the creation and fall, we find the story of Cain and Abel. The story is famous for its murder, but the occasion of the murder was the sacrificial "offering" made to God by both brothers, Cain's from his harvest and Abel's from his livestock (Gen 4:3–5). Thus, the custom of ritual sacrifice appears already well established in humanity's second generation. By ritually offering the fruits of their labors to God, early men fulfilled the cosmic ordering of work to worship. From the first two generations, then, the scriptures present mankind as liturgical by nature—*homo liturgicus.*

Abel's sacrifice is the first of many in the scriptural record. When Noah prepared his ark before the flood, God commanded him to gather "seven pairs of all clean animals" (Gen 7:2)—that is, animals that were suitable for sacrifice. Indeed, when the flood waters subsided, the first thing Noah did was build an altar and sacrifice an exemplar of "every clean animal and every clean bird" as "burnt offerings on the altar" (Gen 8:20).

Abraham followed after the example of his ancestors; and in the long recounting of his life Genesis includes many instances of liturgical worship. Immediately upon his arrival in the promised land, he built altars and called on the name of the Lord (12:7–8). These actions helped set the stage for his ultimate priestly act: the willing offering of his son Isaac at God's command (Gen 22). This, too, he carried forward with ritual precision until the angel of God stayed his hand.

Like Abraham, the later patriarchs also offered sacrifice and performed priestly acts. Jacob, for example, constructed an altar stone and consecrated it by anointing (Gen 28:18). Indeed, throughout the Book of Genesis, liturgy was the province of the patriarchs themselves. In each household, priesthood belonged to the father, who passed the office to his son, ideally the firstborn, by pronouncing a blessing over him. In every household, fathers offered sacrifices and served as mediators between God and their families. In Genesis, we find no evidence of a separate priestly institution. There is no special priestly caste; there is no temple set aside as the exclusive site of sacrifice. Rather, the patriarchs themselves build altars and present offerings at places and times of their own discretion.

The liturgical current continues throughout the Pentateuch. Wenham, an evangelical Protestant, observed that "the sheer bulk of ritual law in the Pentateuch indicates its importance to the biblical writers."[6] He added that the closest modern analogue—in terms of pervasive cultural influence and communicative power—is television. In biblical religion, liturgy represents the medium and the message of God's self-revelation.[7]

The exodus of the Hebrews from Egypt was ordered not so much to liberty as to liturgy. Indeed, God's first command did not require mass emigration, but merely a brief respite from the people's hard labor: "hold a feast to me in the wilderness" (Ex 5:1). Moses then asked Pharaoh to grant the people "a three days' journey into the wilderness, [to] sacrifice to the Lord our God" (Ex 5:3). The feast and the sacrifice were, of course, public acts of ritual worship. They were liturgical actions. A sacrificial feast in God's presence was a meal shared with God, a communion between God and his people.

God's command for observance of the Passover stands as a profound example of liturgical rubric (Ex 12). The ritual was minutely prescribed, from the choice of the lamb to the painting of the doorposts to the communal meal. The liturgy culminated in the Israelites' passing through the Red Sea, which Maly sees as "a grand liturgical procession."[8]

Israel's drama in the desert also turned on liturgy. God clearly instructed his people regarding the place and the manner of right worship, detailing the vestments of the priests down to the last ornament and even the crafting of the curtains for the sanctuary. God's law is far more liturgical than ethical in its emphases. Exodus relates the giving of the Ten Commandments in a single short chapter (20)—with far less space than it gives, for example, to the curtains and frame of the tabernacle (26). Similar attention is given to other liturgical accessories: the ark of the covenant (25), lamps and lampstands (25), veils and altars (27, 30), and priestly vestments (28). Once the narrative lays out all the prescriptions for Israel's liturgy, it then repeats them all (beginning in chapter 35) as it shows the Israelites carrying out God's command! Leviticus and Numbers are similarly concerned—or, more accurately, consumed—with the regulation of Israel's ritual public worship, its liturgy.

Liturgy's dominance continued, of course, as Israel emerged from its wandering in the desert. We can see this especially in the conquest of Jericho. Joshua conquered not so much by military might as by his faithful fulfillment of the Lord's liturgical command. Indeed, the crossing of the Jordan River is depicted as a procession (Jos 4:15–24); and the first actions taken by the Israelites are the ritual circumcision of all males and the prescribed observance of the Passover (Jos 5).

Immediately afterward, when Joshua initiated the battle at Jericho, his attack followed a sabbatical pattern, and it was led not by military officers but by levitical priests. Every day for seven days, the priests processed around the city carrying the ark of the covenant, while armed men blew trumpets continually (Jos 6). The trumpet represented a call not to battle, but to worship. On the seventh day, the walls fell, and Israel destroyed the city.

The purpose of the conquest was not merely dominion, but ultimately the establishment of orderly worship. In the same way, the kingdom-building of David, in its time, was less about the amassing of an empire than the construction of a temple—a "house of prayer for all nations," whose worship would be supervised by Solomon, the Son of David. We find this concern for liturgical correctness expressed especially in the works of the Chronicler, who in First Chronicles 23–25 and 28 portrays David as a genius of liturgical reform, reorganizing the Levites into choirs and establishing new forms and ministries for prayer, sacrifice, and music. In Chronicles, "the cultus emerges as a principle reason for the monarchy's very existence and takes precedence over the Davidic monarchy as the real concern of the Chronicler."[9]

In the Jerusalem temple, priests offered prayers and sacrifices every day on behalf of the nation, the king, and individuals who came to atone for sins, give thanksgiving for blessings, or pray for particular personal intentions. The temple, itself an architectural marvel, was decorated lavishly. Its rites were elaborate, accompanied by chanted and instrumental music. Some of the verses preserved in the biblical Psalms probably originated in the temple liturgies. When later kings of Israel, Hezekiah and Josiah, wanted to initiate moral and societal reform, they began by commanding a reverent observance of the Passover (2 Chr 30 and 35).

The prophets lived in this religious milieu. Liturgical imagery and poetry dominated their visionary passages—think only of Isaiah, Ezekiel, and Daniel. They "saw" the historical implications of liturgy and they revealed what they saw. They saw the worship of heaven and bequeathed it as a model for earth. Their canticles have endured for millennia in the daily and festal prayer of both Jews and Christians.

Liturgical motifs are present as well in the wisdom literature.[10] Sirach personifies Wisdom's existence as a pilgrimage
from creation through the exodus to the establishment of the
temple in Jerusalem (Sir 24). The Book of Wisdom echoes
these historical motifs (Wis 10), culminating in a liturgical
image of Israel's victory: "they sang hymns, O Lord, to thy
holy name, and praised with one accord thy defending hand"
(10:20). Even Job, a gentile, is depicted as offering daily
prayer and sacrifices on behalf of his children: "he would rise
early in the morning and offer burnt offerings according to
the number of them all" (Job 1:5).

The New Testament authors assume all the liturgical
heritage of Israel and show Jesus and his disciples as active
participants in the rites. Jesus made pilgrimages to Jerusalem
(Jn 7:10–14). He regularly attended synagogue (Lk 4:16)
and read and explicated the scriptures there (Lk 4:17–21,
Jn 6:59). He kept the Passover and other Jewish feasts.
He prayed the ancient prayers in the customary ways (Mk
12:29). He underwent a ritual bathing in the Jordan River
(Lk 3:21). He himself established a ritual meal to be observed ever afterward by his followers (Lk 22:19). He instructed his apostles to baptize believers according to a
certain formula (Mt 28:19).

The gospels simultaneously look back to the liturgies of
the Jews and forward to the emerging Christian rites. Luke's
gospel, though written by a gentile, shows a keen sensitivity
to Jewish liturgy. His narrative begins in the temple with the
story of the priest Zechariah and his ministry in the sanctuary, specifically the offering of incense (Lk 1:8–10). Mark's

gospel, on the other hand, repeatedly evokes "the breaking of the bread" and portrays Jesus as using actions that were probably already well established in Christian liturgy. In both stories of the multiplication of loaves (Mk 6:34ff and 8:1ff), notes Eugene LaVerdiere, Jesus is shown "taking bread, blessing (6:41) or giving thanks (8:6), breaking the bread, and giving it to the hungry."[11]

Of all the gospels, John presents the most pervasive liturgical concerns. The narrative unfolds according to the calendar of Jewish feasts; pilgrimage to Jerusalem provides the itinerary for ministry; the climactic moments arrive at or near three celebrations of Passover (chapters 2, 6, and 12). Throughout the gospel, John draws from a profound knowledge of Jewish priestly traditions. He seems equally concerned with the Christian sacraments—so concerned that some modern scholars have referred to the fourth gospel as the "Johannine sacramentary."[12] That, in fact, is the title of Raymond Brown's critical study in which he reviewed a century of scholarship related to John's "sacramentalism." In that essay, Brown listed no fewer than twenty-five proposed sacramental references in John's gospel. Evaluating that early essay almost four decades later, he noted that "scholars tend to see symbolic references to baptism in Johannine passages that mention water, and to the eucharist in Johannine passages dealing with meals, bread, wine, and vine."[13] He concluded:

> *The Johannine references to these two sacraments, both the more explicit references and those that are symbolic, are scat-*

tered in scenes throughout the ministry. This seems to fit in with the Gospel's intention to show how the institutions of the Christian life are rooted in what Jesus said and did during his life.

Moreover, among the four Gospels it is to John most of all that we owe the deep Christian understanding of the purpose of baptism and the eucharist.[14]

In the Acts of the Apostles and the apostolic letters, we find that, in ritual matters, the first Christians followed Christ's example and his commands. They baptized; they held liturgies; they broke bread and prayed (Acts 2:42); they ordained men for ministry by the laying on of hands; they anointed the sick and pronounced ritual forgiveness of sins (Jas 5:14–16). Peter spoke of the church as a priesthood called to "offer sacrifices acceptable to God through Jesus Christ" (1 Pet 2:5). Hebrews quotes Psalm 50, verse 23 to encourage a continual "sacrifice of praise" (Heb 13:15) in the church. The first Christians were no less "God's liturgical people" (to borrow Maly's phrase) than were the tribes of ancient Israel.[15]

The Pauline letters reflect this renewed liturgical milieu. Paul assumes that his letters will be read in the assembly *(ekklesia,* church), and he concerns himself often with both the liturgical expressions and the inner dispositions of worshipers. These themes dominate 1 Corinthians 10–11, of course; but they inform many other passages as well. Recent scholarship, across denominational lines, has examined Paul's use of technical cultic terms such as *leitourgia* (liturgy; e.g.,

Phil 2:17), *eucharistia* (thanksgiving, eucharist; e.g., 2 Cor 9:11), *thusia* (sacrifice; e.g., Phil 4:18), *hierourgein* (priestly service; e.g., Rom 15:16), and *prosphoron* (offering; e.g., Rom 15:16), concluding that Paul's usages have sometimes suffered misunderstanding in translation and interpretation.[16]

Proceeding further into the New Testament, we find material that is increasingly and more explicitly liturgical. Hebrews is an extended meditation on the liturgy of Israel and the liturgy of the church, the liturgy of heaven and the liturgy on earth. The author invokes many of the ancient rites and sacrifices, from those of Abel, Abraham, and Melchizedek to those of Aaron, the Levites, and the high priest in the last days of the Herodian temple. He is especially concerned with the sin offerings and the liturgy of the feast of Yom Kippur. He then goes on to show the ancient feasts' typological fulfillment in Christ and in the assembly *(ekklesia, church)*—"the city of the living God, the heavenly Jerusalem, and to innumerable angels in festal gathering, and to the assembly of the firstborn who are enrolled in heaven . . . and to Jesus, the mediator of a new covenant, and to the sprinkled blood that speaks more graciously than the blood of Abel" (Heb 12:22–24).[17]

Perhaps no book of the Bible is as densely packed with liturgical images and texts as the last book of the Bible. The book begins with the reading of scrolls (chs. 2–3) and ends with the "marriage supper of the Lamb" (Rev 19:9). Important action takes place around heaven's altar (8:3). The *dramatis personae* include robed priests (4:4). Liturgical accouterments abound—candles (1:12), incense (5:8), and chalices (ch. 16)—as do canticles and acclamations from both Jewish and Christian liturgy: the *Sanctus* (4:8), the *Gloria* (15:3–4), the *Alleluia* (19:1, 3, 6). Trumpets accompany the sacred action (8:7, 9:1, etc.), as they accompanied the liturgy in Jerusalem's temple. In the eastern churches, the Book of Revelation is called a veritable "icon of the liturgy." We will return to the Apocalypse and Hebrews for closer study at the end of this book.

From Genesis to Revelation, the texts themselves demonstrate the formal unity of scripture and liturgy. Scripture is, by and large, *about* liturgy. Often, it is liturgy—or the culpable neglect of liturgy—that drives the biblical drama. Liturgy sustains the assembly of God's people—the *qahal*, the *ekklesia*, the *church*—and liturgy restores it when it falls. Maly put it memorably. Israel's sanctification, he wrote,

> *was achieved in a positive way through the divine liturgy. If the people of God had, through that abandonment of the covenant that had brought on the exile, lost their right to be considered God's own community, they could only regain that right by experiencing anew the saving acts of God. This new creation was accomplished in the liturgy.*[18]

The Formal Relationship— The Bible Is for Liturgy

Liturgy and scripture possess a formal unity as well. The Bible was made for liturgical use. Carroll Stuhlmueller spoke quite simply of "the scriptures as liturgical documents of Old and New Testament times."[19] In some cases—certain Psalms, for instance—this is self-evident. They are antiphonal or responsory chants that presume a ritual setting and a worshiping assembly. Gerard Sloyan observed, "The scripture came into existence as part of the life of a worshipping community. . . . There can be no doubt whatever that liturgical influences were strong in the formation and even the actual writing of large sections of both testaments."[20]

But it is in the Bible as a whole that we find the true material unity of scripture and liturgy. For both the Old and New Testaments were canonized not for private study so much as public reading. The canon—the formal and definitive collection of sacred writings—formed gradually and closed relatively late in the history of both Jews and Christians. Indeed, there seem to have been many incremental "canonizations" along the way to the definitive closing of the canon. For Jews, the date is traditionally set at the end of the first century or the beginning of the second century of our era. For Christians, the New Testament list solidified with the synods of Hippo and Carthage (393, 397, and 419 A.D.).

The scriptural canon was enacted primarily as a "rule" for the liturgy. The Greek word *kanon* means, literally, a measuring stick. From the late fourth century onward, Christians used the word to describe the church's official lists that determined a document's fitness for use in public worship. "The term is late and Christian," writes Eugene Ulrich, "though the idea is Jewish."[21]

The rule dictated liturgical use. Yet it was surely liturgical use that preceded (and determined) the rule. The church promulgated its final New Testament canon with the local councils of Hippo (393 A.D.) and Carthage (397 and 417), whose acts were confirmed and ratified by Pope Damasus I. By then, however, the church had been celebrating the eucharistic liturgy for more than three centuries; and the earliest patristic evidence shows that the liturgy always made use of sacred scripture. As Everett Ferguson points out: "The church did not have to wait until the end of the second century (and certainly not the fourth century) to know what books to read in church."[22]

Thus, in an interesting historical turnabout, liturgical use became a primary criterion for compiling the canon that would officially limit the books deemed suitable for liturgical use. It is one of the classic examples of *lex orandi, lex credendi*—the law of worship dictating the law of belief.

P. J. Tomson traced the process of canonization, observing that "early Christians followed Jewish custom . . . in distinguishing hidden books, *apokrupha,* from *phanera biblia* or public books. . . . Now this terminology reflects the behavioural basis of canon debates, namely, selecting which books or passages are to be out during public worship and which are not." He went on to explain that canonization created a "reading community" that read in a festive way, a fact implicit in the Hebrew words for both synagogue *(edah)* and church-assembly *(qahal).* "Prayers, chants, sacrifices, or public addresses were common ingredients, but the reading out of books was found nowhere else—except that the *Ecclesia* simply followed the *Synagoga* here." Tomson added that canonization for liturgy established a new hermeneutic for the assembly—with officiating clergy as authoritative interpreters and a presumed interrelatedness of the canon's component books.[23]

Liturgical use was not the only criterion for canonicity; the councils also considered apostolicity, orthodoxy, and catholicity. But the conciliar decrees were, in a sense, confirmation of a fait accompli. Ferguson writes: "The councils of the church played little part in the canonization of scripture. When councils did speak on the subject, their voice was a ratification of what had already become the mind of the church." And, we might add, its public voice.

Use, then, determined canon every bit as much as canon eventually would determine use. Ferguson adds: "Distinctive worship practices . . . served as preconditions for a canon of scripture. The eucharist involved the remembrance of the passion of Christ and particularly the institution narrative."[24] Long before any conciliar decree, the words of scripture were "canonized" by repeated liturgical use.[25]

The Old Testament itself records several moments of scriptural canonization; and it is interesting to note that they all take place in liturgical settings. Consider Moses' giving of the law, as described in Exodus. It is worth quoting at length.

Moses came and told the people all the words of the Lord and all the ordinances; and all the people answered with one voice, and said, "All the words which the Lord has spoken we will do." And Moses wrote all the words of the Lord.

And he rose early in the morning, and built an altar at the foot of the mountain, and twelve pillars, according to the twelve tribes of Israel. And he sent young men of the people of Israel, who offered burnt offerings and sacrificed peace offerings of oxen to the Lord. And Moses took half of the blood and put it in basins, and half of the blood he threw against the altar. Then he took the book *of the covenant [emphasis mine], and read it in the hearing of the people; and they said, "All that the Lord has spoken we will do, and we will be obedient." And Moses took the blood and threw it upon the people, and said, "Behold the blood of the covenant which the Lord has made with you in accordance with all these words." (Ex 24:3–8)*

Moses recorded God's law and, in doing so, created a sort of "canon," and each stage took place within an elaborate liturgy involving proclamation and sacrifice.

The Second Book of Kings portrays the reformer Josiah as rediscovering the long-neglected book of the law and then reestablishing its authority with a liturgy. He called a great assembly "and he read in their hearing all the words of the book of the covenant" (2 Kgs 23:2). The reading was followed by a ritual cleansing of the Jerusalem temple.

Similarly, on return from the exile, the priest Ezra reintroduced the scriptures to the people. "From early morning to midday," he read the law of Moses aloud to the assembly, in an unmistakably liturgical setting. "And Ezra opened the book in the sight of all the people, for he was above all the people; and when he opened it all the people stood. And Ezra blessed the Lord the great God; and all the people answered, 'Amen, Amen,' lifting up their hands; and they bowed their heads and worshiped the Lord with their faces to the ground" (Neh 8:3, 5–6).

In the same way, in the New Testament, moments in the canonical process come within liturgical contexts. It is in the Emmaus story, as we have seen, that Christ opens up "all the scriptures"—thus validating the Old Testament books and establishing a model for Christian interpretation. The conclusion of the Book of Revelation, which declares the book prophetic and unalterable (Rev 22:18–19), is another moment of "canonization," and it follows immediately upon a dazzling array of liturgical scenes, culminating in the marriage supper of the Lamb.

Scripture is canonized for liturgy, and it is liturgy that canonizes scripture. Eusebius relates an illuminating story from the second century of the Christian era, a time when the church's canon was still largely a local matter and had some elasticity. The bishop of Antioch, Serapion, was called upon to settle a dispute between Christian factions in the nearby city of Rhossus. He asked the parties to make peace, if necessary, by permitting one faction to read the apocryphal Gospel of Peter in church. "If this is all that makes your petty quarrel," he declared, "why, then, let it be read." Serapion himself had not examined Pseudo-Peter, but he had assumed it was orthodox. Other bishops informed him otherwise, however, and, after studying the text of Pseudo-Peter, Serapion rescinded his earlier decision. In his decree, he informed the Christians of Rhossus that the supposed gospel lacked apostolicity and smacked of the docetist heresy.[26]

In this one story, from early Christian antiquity, we can see the interplay of the many qualities that would eventually become criteria for determining canonicity: apostolicity, orthodoxy, and catholicity. What brought them all together, though, was a liturgical decree and its eventual withdrawal. Serapion, believing "Peter" to be authentic, granted it "canonical" status by allowing it to be read in the assembly. Finding it deficient, he retracted his decision and denied "Peter" any lasting place in the liturgy, as had his fellow bishops.

All this took place before the word "canon" had yet been applied to the scriptural contents. Yet the material unity of scripture and liturgy was already strong and ready to withstand testing.

The bond uniting scripture and liturgy is indissoluble. What establishes and constitutes that bond is the subject of the next chapter.

CHAPTER 4

❧❧

COVENANT: THE BOND
OF UNITY

I F SCRIPTURE AND liturgy exist in an indissoluble unity, it is because of the strength of the bond that unites them. That bond is the *covenant*—in Hebrew, *b'rith;* in Greek, *diatheke.* In the second century, Irenaeus observed that to understand "the divine program and economy for the salvation of humanity" it is necessary first to understand God's "several covenants with humanity" and also "the special character of each covenant."[1] The canonical scriptures themselves are traditionally divided into old covenant and new covenant. At the Last Supper, Christ identifies Christianity's *defining liturgical act,* the eucharist, as "the new covenant in my blood" (Lk 22:20). In the words of Old Testament scholar Walter Bruggemann, "Biblical faith is essentially covenantal in its perception of all reality."[2]

Covenant, then, serves as an interpretive key to understanding scripture and liturgy and their interrelations. Even a cursory examination of related texts will demonstrate that both liturgy and scripture serve as means to a common end, which is the establishment, renewal, and maintenance of a covenant relationship.

And what exactly is a covenant relationship? It is a family

bond. Frank Moore Cross of Harvard describes covenant as the "legal means by which the duties and privileges of kinship may be extended to another individual or group, including aliens."[3] Covenant, then, creates a *family bond* where none had previously existed. Two examples familiar to modern readers would be marriage and adoption.

The scriptures present examples of many types of covenant. There are human covenants: covenants between men, such as Jacob and Laban (Gen 31:44–54) or David and Jonathan (1 Sam 18:3, 20:8); and treaty covenants between tribes and nations (e.g., 1 Kgs 20:34). More important, however, are the divine covenants, God's "several covenants with humanity." Yet all of these covenants—human and divine, between persons and between nations—were alike in that they formed new family bonds, and ever afterward the covenanting parties spoke of one another in terms of kinship (see 1 Sam 20:14–17). Cross remarks that, although "often it has been asserted that the language of 'brotherhood' and 'fatherhood,' 'love,' and 'loyalty' is 'covenant terminology,' " this is "to turn things upside down. The language of covenant, kinship-in-law, is taken from the language of kinship, kinship-in-flesh."

This has profound implications for the divine covenants. For they must, then, represent a familial bond between God and human beings. The scriptures bear this out. God promises the Davidic king: "You are my son, today I have begotten you" (Ps 2:7). God says of Solomon: "I will be a father to him, and he will become my son" (2 Sam 8:14). In other passages, God applies this family relationship to all Israel (see Hos 11:1). As a result of the divine covenants, Israel became 'am Yahweh, which is usually translated as "the people of God," but literally means the "family of God" or "God's kindred." Yahweh, according to Cross, "is the god of Israel, the Divine Kinsman, the god of the covenant."

Covenant-making followed certain patterns throughout the ancient Near East. The biblical covenants resemble covenants made in neighboring societies: Babylonian, Hittite, Assyrian, and even Greek and Roman. Among the common elements the most important was certainly the solemn ritual oath, by which the covenant was ratified. The oath marked something more than a promise. It was, to borrow J. L. Austin's phrase, a "speech-act." Austin noted that, while most words are merely descriptive, there are certain phrases that really accomplish what they describe (e.g., "I declare war"; "You're fired"; "I dub thee knight"). Once they are uttered, they perform actions. Thus, philosophers call such phrases "performative utterances."

In covenant oaths, the two parties invoked God as witness and guarantor on their agreement. "When an oath is taken, God is in attendance," wrote Rabbi Jacob Neusner; ". . . [T]he oath serves, within the Israelite polity, to engage God's participation within the transactions of Israelites, to involve God in Israel's points of inner conflict, to ask God to impart certainty."[4] By swearing in the presence of God, the two parties invited divine blessings upon fulfillment of the conditions of the covenant, and curses upon non-fulfillment. They often sealed the covenant with a ritual action, such as a sacrifice, a meal, or some other sign. God's covenant with Abraham was sealed by circumcision, the cutting of the male's foreskin. Over time, the sign became so closely associated with the covenant as to be synonymous with it. Thus, New Testament texts refer to Jews as "the covenant of circumcision" (Acts 7:8) and sometimes simply "the circumcision" (Col 4:11). Similarly, Jesus equated the sign of his covenant with the covenant that it sealed: "This cup . . . is the new covenant in my blood" (Lk 22:20). And so the cup *was* the covenant. In these instances, both the covenantal sign and the covenanting persons are equated with the covenant itself.

In the Bible's classic covenants, we find all of the basic elements. We find the establishment of an interpersonal, familial bond: "And I will walk among you, and will be your God, and you shall be my people" [literally, "my kindred"] (Lev 26:12, see also Dt 32:6, 8, 18–19; Jer 30:22; Ezek 36:28). We find also the consequences that follow from fidelity or infidelity to the covenant: "I have set before you life and death, blessing and curse; therefore choose life, that you and your descendants may live" (Dt 30:19). And frequently we find ritual sacrifice. The sacrifices, however, were not intended merely to destroy a life, but rather to sustain a new family life. With the exception of the whole burnt offering, no sacrifice was complete until the victim was consumed in a ritual meal—even when one of the covenanting parties was God. The great Torah scholar Rabbi Baruch Levine describes all the sacrifices prescribed in Leviticus as etiquette for meals in the presence of God.[5] The meal was a familial communion between God and man.

The ritual action sealed the covenant at the moment the agreement was made. Periodically in the future, the terms of the covenant would be read aloud in a ceremony of covenant renewal. The Passover, for example, was a one-time historical event experienced by the Hebrews when they were slaves in Egypt. The Passover meal, however, was celebrated annually as a liturgical remembrance and renewal of the covenant.

Again, this pattern was similar across Near Eastern cultures. M. G. Kline points out that it was customary for covenant-treaty texts "to be deposited in the presence of a god, carefully guarded, and periodically read publicly in the vassal kingdom."[6] This represents a kind of documentary canonization that was standard in covenant-making. Kline goes so far as to say that "Canon is inherent in covenant."[7] Indeed, the scriptures are canonized precisely so that they will be preserved for liturgical and memorial proclamation.

Oswald Loretz put it simply: "the canon is derived from the covenant of God with Israel." "[T]he canonical writings of the Old Testament . . . can only be understood when they are viewed against the background of the covenant."[8]

In this context, it is interesting to note that only at a relatively late date (the end of the fourth century) was the Greek word *kanon* applied to the list of biblical books. Earlier in the fourth century, Eusebius had employed a different term for canonicity. The writings that were then acknowledged by the church, he said, were "encovenanted"—*endiathekai*.[9] The sacred texts were, for the church in the fourth century, *the covenantal documents,* kept in God's presence in the sanctuary, for the purpose of liturgical remembrance.[10]

So we see that covenant is a familial bond that inheres in a certain rule, or canon.[11] The covenant is embodied by its law, or canonical scripture. The covenant is embodied also by its liturgy (e.g., the "Roman Canon"). As the canon is integral to the keeping of a covenant, so the liturgy is essential to the ratification and renewal of the covenant. Indeed, we may say that the covenant is embodied in its liturgical sign, as in the case of circumcision or the eucharistic cup. The covenant is embodied as well in the covenanting persons: "I have given you as a covenant to the people" (see Is 42:6).

The Hebrew scriptures describe many covenants, some human, some divine. Some of them stand out as particularly important, especially in relation to the three "mountain peaks" we noted in salvation history—creation, exodus, and kingdom. We may mention, for example, the divine covenants with creation, with Noah, with Abraham, with Moses, and with David. Each successive covenant was really a renewal of the primeval "cosmic covenant." But each, in succession, extended membership in God's family to a greater number of people: what was first given to a couple was then extended to a household, then a tribe, then a nation, and finally a kingdom. And with each successive covenant came a re-templing, a re-appropriation of the scriptures—a renewed law and renewed order of worship. "For when there is a change in the priesthood, there is necessarily a change in the law as well" (Heb 7:12).

Creation—The Cosmic Covenant

We have already noted how the Genesis accounts of creation evoke cultic activity, sacred time, and priestly office. In the beginning, God created the heavens and the earth in a cosmic liturgy, and he appointed Adam as high priest with dominion over creation. In all his earthly activity, Adam served in a priestly role, and all his work was directed to worship, because God had *hallowed* the seventh day.

Ancient traditions of biblical interpretation look upon this divine action as a "Great Oath,"[12] an oath that bound the wild forces of nature, an earth that "was without form and void" (Gen 1:2). According to *Sifre Deuteronomy,* a Jewish commentary compiled in the third century: "When the Holy One, blessed be he, created, he did not create . . . except by an oath."[13] The contemporary theologian Robert Murray has called this oath the "cosmic covenant."[14] Recent Catholic magisterial documents have referred to the same reality as "the first covenant" *(Dies Domini* 8). "Thus the revelation of creation is inseparable from the revelation and forging of the covenant of the one God with his People" (CCC, n. 288).[15]

Where, precisely, does God swear his covenant oath? He does so in the very act of hallowing the seventh day (Gen 2:2). The seventh day itself is God's Great Oath.

While etymologies do not often make for good exegesis, the etymology of the Hebrew word for "seven" is essential for our understanding of the Genesis text. For it is from the "seventh day" of creation that all subsequent covenant oaths took their origin and inspiration.

The Hebrew word for the number seven, *sheva,* also has a verb form. *Shava* is the verb for swearing a covenant oath.

Its literal meaning is "to seven oneself." When human beings swear in this way, they follow the precedent set by God at the dawn of creation. Throughout the Old Testament, the number seven will recur many times in connection with the making of covenants and the offering of covenant sacrifices. For example, the place of Abraham's covenant oath with Abimelech was later named *Beer-sheva,* which is alternately translated as "Well of the Seven" or "Well of the Oath." It was there that Abraham swore his oath and gave seven ewe lambs as guarantee (Gen 21:22–34).

In Genesis 2, the seventh day was the sign of the covenant that God had made with a man and a woman, Adam and Eve, though also with their offspring in every generation—on the condition that the primal couple remain faithful to his expressed commandment: "of the tree of the knowledge of good and evil you shall not eat" (Gen 2:17). Adam and Eve, of course, failed to keep this single command and forfeited their covenant kinship with God.[16]

With the failure of the covenant with Adam came increasing moral decay and a corresponding unbinding of the cosmic forces. The resulting chaos culminated in the great flood (Gen 7). After the flood, God renewed his cosmic covenant, this time with the household of the righteous Noah. Thus, the covenant grew wider in its application: From a couple, it now expanded to an extended family, parents and offspring. And both liturgy and law underwent significant developments. After the floodwaters subsided, Noah gave thanks by presiding over a sacrifice of "clean animals" on Mount Ararat.

God raised a rainbow in the sky as a "sign of the covenant" (9:17) with Noah's household. He gave them a brief moral and dietary law to follow (Gen 8:20–9:17).

Exodus—The Covenants with Abraham and Moses

The history of the divine covenant unfolds with another renewal in Genesis, represented by God's dealings with the chieftain Abraham and his household. Though Abram was childless at the beginning of the story, God promised him a vast tribe of descendants (Gen 15:5). So, again, we see a further extension of God's covenant family.

God revealed himself to Abram in Chaldean Ur and called him to inhabit the land of Canaan, far distant from his home. Abram's vocation evokes that of Adam, in that God expects both men to fill the land and subdue it (compare Gen 1:28 and 12:1–3). As the sabbath was the sign of the cosmic covenant and the rainbow the sign of the Noahic covenant, the distinguishing mark of the Abrahamic covenant was the ritual circumcision of every male in Abraham's family.

God's commandments to Abraham—to inhabit the land and to circumcise all males—constituted, with Abraham's sacrificial customs, a new "canon" for God's covenant family: a renewed liturgy and law. God promised his own everlasting fidelity to the covenant, but revealed to Abraham that future generations would break the bond, with devastating consequences: "Know of a surety that your descendants will be sojourners in a land that is not theirs, and will be slaves there, and they will be oppressed for four hundred years, but I will bring judgment on the nation which they serve, and afterward they shall come out with great possessions" (Gen 15:13).

Thus the stage was set for the exodus—Israel's deliverance from slavery in Egypt—which was itself the occasion for yet another covenant renewal. This time, Moses stood as mediator between God and God's chosen people, the twelve tribes descended from the sons of the patriarch Jacob (Israel). As Moses led the tribes out of slavery in Egypt, God ratified a covenant that made Israel a nation of priests (Ex 19:6). God's covenant family was now a populous nation. The sign of the covenant with Moses was the Passover, the sacrificial meal that transformed the tribes into God's national family. God gave the ten commandments and other statutes to Moses so that Israel would have its own national constitution.

Jews and Christians honor Moses as "the Lawgiver," because he received God's covenant law and conveyed it to Israel. Tradition credits him with authorship of the entire Torah, the book of the law and the primary canon of the Bible. But Moses was as much a giver of liturgy as of law; and, indeed, entire chapters of the law treat the most minute aspects of liturgy (see Ex 25–31). Moses oversaw the re-templing of Israel in the construction of the tabernacle and the ark of the covenant—a new place of worship, a new object of veneration, and a full festal liturgical calendar.[17] After Israel sinned by worshiping the golden calf, Moses also supervised the reordering of the priesthood, with the tribe of Levi assuming the office that God had originally intended for all the nation.

To the Mosaic covenant, then, tradition assigned a Mosaic canon of scripture and a Mosaic liturgy, the Torah of Moses and the worship at the tabernacle.

Kingdom—The Covenant with the House of David

In the last great covenant renewal of the Old Testament, God established a bond with King David and his royal house. God covenanted with David to build a worldwide kingdom (see Pss 2 and 72), whose sign would be the everlasting throne of David's son (see Ps 89:3–4 and Ps 110:4). Now the covenant family grew from the nation of Israel to a newly established *kingdom,* whose monarch was destined to rule over all the nations. David and his son, Solomon, carried out God's plan by incorporating many of the surrounding nations and city-states into the covenant, by treaty and by intermarriage. Since kings take tribute from subject nations, this also meant that foreigners would make annual visits to Jerusalem, whose temple was considered "a house of prayer for all nations." From the temple God would receive the prayers of gentiles as well as Israelites (see 2 Chron 6:32–33).

Under the rule of David and Solomon, the sacrificial system was adapted from the wandering tabernacle of the exodus to the Jerusalem temple. David took a special interest in revitalizing the liturgy. Jewish tradition reveres him as a sort of second lawgiver; but his special "law" was dominated by liturgy. Says the *Midrash Tehillim,* the oldest surviving commentary on the Psalms: "Moses gave Israel the five books [of the Law], and David gave Israel the five books of the Psalms."[18] The same notion appears in Hippolytus, who wrote the oldest surviving Christian commentary on the Psalms.[19] The Psalms, the prophets, and the wisdom books stand as a Davidic canon—legal, sapiential, universal in their appeal, and overwhelmingly liturgical.

⟐

What distinguishes the Davidic canon? Hartmut Gese, Harvey Guthrie, and others have detected a distinct character represented by the type of worship offered in the Jerusalem temple.[20] They observe that with the shift from Sinai to Zion—from the Mosaic covenant to the Davidic—comes a corresponding shift from the sin offering to the thank offering (in Hebrew, *todah*). Gese noted that "the thank offering constituted the cultic basis for the main bulk of the Psalms."[21] Timothy Gray went so far as to speak of the "todah shape of the Psalter."[22] The words of the Psalms themselves seem to record this shift: "Sacrifice and offering thou dost not desire. . . . Burnt offering and sin offering thou hast not required" (Ps 40:6). "Offer to God a *sacrifice of thanksgiving* [emphasis mine], and pay your vows to the Most High" (Ps 50:14).

The *todah* was a sacrifice of bread and wine, usually offered by an individual in thanksgiving for deliverance from

65

some grave peril. The worshiper also sang a "new song" to commemorate his rescue and recount God's marvelous deeds; several of the Psalms seem to fit this liturgical form (e.g., Pss 9, 50, 51, 56, 66, 69). The *todah* had existed in the law of Moses (see Lev 7:12ff), but it came to dominate Israel's spirituality only with David's ascendancy. Yet it would have a lasting effect on the history of spirituality. In the first centuries of the common era, two of the most revered Jewish commentators, Philo of Alexandria and Aquila, would examine the *todah* under its equivalent term in Greek: *eucharistia*.[23] So central was the *todah* to the spirit of biblical religion after David that the ancient rabbis held that "In the coming [messianic] age, all sacrifices will cease except the *todah* sacrifice. This will never cease in all eternity."[24]

Key, then, to David's covenant is the remembrance of God's mighty deeds—salvific deeds—in the dominant liturgical form used in the temple. The last of the Old Testament covenants brings Israel's religion to its most universal expression thus far, providing an opportunity for even the gentiles to worship the true God (at the temple) and grasp God's law (through the wisdom books).

There can be no doubt that the nascent Christian church saw itself as heir to this patrimony of covenantal worship. The Greek term most often used to describe the rites of the covenants is *mysterion*—in English, *mystery*. We find the term in both the New Testament and the Septuagint version of the Old Testament. *Mysterion* often refers to something "hidden," as when Paul described the hidden purpose of the cosmos and history. The term was also frequently applied to Hellenistic and Eastern cults that involved secret rituals of initiation and advancement: the so-called "mystery religions."

The Latins, however, chose not to translate *mysterion* with its cognate, *mysterium,* but rather with a legal term, *sacramentum.* The Latin term denoted Roman society's most sacred oaths—for example, the imperial military oath, which was permanently binding and affected all aspects of one's life, from matters of conscience to clothing and place of residence. The *sacramentum* transferred a Roman male's primary allegiance from the family to the legion, which became for him a new family. Solemnly sworn, all-encompassing, and binding for life, the Roman *sacramentum* was the functional equivalent of the Israelite *b'rith,* covenant.

Sacramentum was so much a part of early Christian life that one of the earliest pagan observers, Pliny the Younger (112 A.D.), used the word to describe the essential rite of the Christians, the eucharistic liturgy, in which worshipers "bound themselves by oath" *(cum sacramento obstringere)* to refrain from sin.[25] The Christian Tertullian, a lawyer himself, followed this usage, as do the later exegetes, such as Jerome.[26]

There are shades of difference between *mysterion* and *sacramentum,* but they are differences of emphasis and not of substance. The former emphasizes the hidden, supernatural reality behind the covenantal rites; the latter emphasizes the visible rites themselves. *Sacramentum* emphasizes the sign, *mysterion* the signified.[27]

But, again, these are differences of emphasis, and they should not be exaggerated. Both the Greek and Latin terms have profoundly covenantal implications. It is interesting to note, in this context, that the ancient pagan cults that boasted of their "mysteries"—the cult of Mithras, for example—also bound their adherents by strict and life-changing oaths, which, again, the Latins understood as *sacramenta*. In the ancient world, it was all of a piece.[28]

Near the end of the second century, Clement of Alexandria, who was probably an initiate of the pagan mysteries before his conversion to Christianity, urged other would-be mystics to enter the covenant with Christ by way of the sacraments: "Then thou shalt have the vision of my God, and shalt be initiated in those holy mysteries, and shalt taste the joys that are hidden away in heaven. . . . O truly sacred mysteries! O pure light! In the blaze of the torches I have a vision of heaven and of God. I become holy by initiation. The Lord reveals the mysteries; He marks the worshiper with His seal. . . . "[29]

It would be difficult for us to exaggerate the importance—indeed the centrality—of the covenant in biblical religion. Alan Segal put it starkly: "The root metaphor underlying Hebrew society is expressed in the word *covenant*."[30] N. T.

Wright observed, in an equally unqualified way: "The idea of covenant was central to Judaism in this [New Testament] period. . . . covenantal ideas were totally common and regular. . . . Covenantal theology was the air breathed by the Judaism of this period."[31]

Segal went on to explain: "The Israelite myth of covenant simply has unique characteristics that allow it to address history along with cosmology. The events of Israelite history itself were interpreted in terms of the root metaphor of the covenant relationship."[32] Following this line of thought, we can see that covenant is the quality most characteristic of God's dealings with mankind. Covenant is the recurring *typos*—the trademark of God, as it were—evident at every stage of history and every exploration of cosmology. For Segal, the typology extends into the future through the liturgy: "Past events are consciously used as liturgical models for the covenantal meaning of human destiny. . . . The Passover liturgy today contains the ancient lines, 'Every Jew should look upon himself as though he too came forth out of Egypt.' "[33]

Covenant, then, must be the master key to any thorough understanding of economy and typology, and to any true mystagogy of the liturgy. The monumental import of God's covenant oaths—sworn to Abraham and David at Moriah and Zion, for the blessing of all nations—is what makes salvation history really and literally *sacramental,* and not simply symbolic. Anscar Vonier noted wisely: "That the Son of God should use the term Covenant in connection with the order of things He came to bring about is sufficient authority to justify us in making of the idea of the Covenant a thing of supreme spiritual importance."[34] Covenant is *the* fundamental element of the Jewish and Christian patrimony; yet it is an element that has somehow slipped away from much modern scholarship, and even modern religion. What Romano Guardini said generations ago still holds true today: "It is strange how completely the idea of the covenant has vanished from the Christian consciousness. We do mention it, but it seems to have lost its meaning for us."[35] The loss is incalculable for those who would interpret the Bible or practice theology.

Lacking all the critical apparatus of today's scholarship, Irenaeus still kept a clearer view of salvation history, because he saw it through the lens of its single most important idea. The "divine economy," he said, turns on the "several covenants." The second-century master saw all the Old Testament covenants as real historical events that typologically prefigured the Christ-event. Using Pauline language, he spoke of all the covenants being "recapitulated" in the new covenant of Jesus Christ.

Each covenant had its canon of law and worship, its proclamation and sacrifice, as would the covenant announced in Luke 22 and 1 Corinthians 11. In recapitulating the covenants that had gone before, Christ abolished none, but renewed them all by fulfilling them perfectly. His covenant created a family bond not merely with a couple, a household, a tribe, a nation, or a kingdom—but with all humanity.

CHAPTER 5

"IN YOUR HEARING":
LITURGICAL PROCLAMATION
OF THE WORD

A DRAMATIC TURNING point in Luke's gospel comes relatively early, when Jesus launches his public ministry (Lk 4:16ff). According to Luke, Jesus announced his mission in the midst of the liturgy, the sabbath liturgy of the synagogue, which it was "his custom" to attend. Jesus "stood up to read," and he received the day's prescribed reading from the prophet Isaiah (Is 61:1–2; 58:6). After reading, "he closed the book, and gave it back to the attendant, and sat down; and the eyes of all in the synagogue were fixed upon him."

Jesus and his hearers were clearly following a familiar liturgical form. The rite employed various ministerial roles and persons; it involved standing and sitting at appointed times, predetermined readings, and commentary on the readings. The familiar setting provides the narrative's dramatic tension and sense of expectation: he "sat down; and the eyes of all . . . were fixed upon him."

Then Jesus preached the homily that established the course of his ministry: "And he began to say to them, 'Today this scripture has been fulfilled in your hearing' " (Lk 4:21). He went on to anticipate his congregation's objections and defend his mission in light of other Hebrew scriptures (1 Kgs 17 and 2 Kgs 5). Unlike the pair of travelers at Emmaus, however, the congregation at Nazareth remained uncomprehending; and, growing enraged, they even attempted to kill Jesus at once. Jesus escaped, and moved on to another town, where Luke immediately portrays him, once again, taking part in a synagogue liturgy (Lk 4:31–33).

The synagogue liturgy in Jesus' time, as in our own time, was non-sacrificial. It was a liturgy of the word—involving scriptural prayer, proclamation, and interpretation. Indeed, it is likely that the Christian liturgy of the word derived from this formative experience of the first generation of Christians, who were predominantly Jews.

It is in the context of the traditional synagogue liturgy that Luke describes something happening. Something that had *not* been before, now actually was. Something was *actualized* in the liturgical proclamation. The actualization, moreover, took place in a specific way: "this scripture has been fulfilled *in your hearing.*"

Despite the congregation's incomprehension, the scripture was fulfilled in their hearing. The fulfillment did not depend upon their response, but upon their liturgical hearing of the proclamation. Here, Jesus followed the pattern that had been established in the liturgical acts of canonization performed by Moses, Josiah, and Ezra. Biblical religion has always required the proclamation of God's word within the assembly of God's people. In the old covenant, that proclamation had always been public, communal, and liturgical. It remained so with the new covenant of Jesus Christ.

Jesus' subsequent preaching placed a particular emphasis on the hearing of the word. In the parable of the sower, Jesus presented a taxonomy of people categorized by what they do "when they hear the word" (Mk 4:13ff). Paul expounded the importance of "hearing" in a rhetorically forceful passage of his Letter to the Romans:

> *But how are men to call upon him in whom they have not believed? And how are they to believe in him of whom they have never heard? And how are they to hear without a preacher? And how can men preach unless they are sent? As it is written, "How beautiful are the feet of those who preach good news!" But they have not all obeyed the gospel; for Isaiah says, "Lord, who has believed what he has heard from us?" So faith comes from what is heard, and what is heard comes by the preaching of Christ. (Rom 10:14–17)*

"So faith comes from what is heard." Or to take another familiar translation of the passage: "faith comes by hearing." Paul would pose the same doctrine in a question to the church in Galatia, "Did you receive the Spirit by works of the law, or by hearing with faith?" (Gal 3:2). The context makes it abundantly clear that Paul intended the obvious answer to be "by hearing."

John the seer confirmed the privileged place of liturgical "hearing" when he pronounced his benediction at the beginning of the Book of Revelation: "Blessed is he who reads aloud the words of the prophecy, and blessed are those who hear, and who keep what is written therein" (Rev 1:3).

Thus, for John, the word must be written down, but its blessing arrives when it is read aloud and heard. Scripture is written for the sake of liturgical proclamation. Its blessing comes within the liturgical assembly.

The scriptures frequently exhort and praise those who faithfully hear the word. We do not need to plumb the depths of mystical theology to find the reasons for this. There are very practical, historical reasons. In antiquity, there was no real mass production of books. A book's distribution depended upon laborious copying by hand, a very expensive and time-consuming project. In the case of the scriptures, moreover, we are talking about not just one book, but many. Few individuals—or even assemblies—could afford to own copies of all the books that could be read in the liturgy, that is, all the canonical scriptures. It is not until late antiquity (the fourth century) that we read of compilations that we might call "Bibles," which include all the books of one or another biblical testament.[1]

Furthermore, literacy varied widely from time to time and place to place. It is likely that, at least in some times and places, congregations were largely unable to read the sacred texts. Anthropologists often distinguish between "orality" and "literacy" in cultures, marking the different ways that societies measure education. In the case of biblical religion, we might rightly speak instead of *aurality*. Scripture is actualized "in your hearing." "Faith comes by hearing." "Blessed are those who hear."

This is not to say that private reading of scripture never occurred in antiquity. In the mid-fourth century, Athanasius acknowledged both "those who read" the biblical books and "those who hear" them instead.[2] A generation later, Theodore of Mopsuestia and his student John Chrysostom also mentioned both liturgical and private reading of the Bible. In his *Commentary on Zephaniah,* Theodore wrote: "All of us, having come to faith in Christ the Lord from the nations, received the Scriptures . . . and now enjoy them, reading them aloud in the churches and keeping them at home."[3] Nor was this a local phenomenon peculiar to Syria or Egypt. The circle of Roman noblewomen who studied with Jerome learned to read not only the Latin translations of scripture, but also the original Greek and Hebrew texts, all of which they owned. Of Melania the Elder, Jerome wrote: "The Bible never left her holy hands." And when Augustine, in northern Italy, heard the playful voices that changed his life forever, the children were calling out, *"Tolle, lege!"*—"Take up and read." And in the comfort of his home, Augustine was able to act on their imperative, taking up Paul's Letter to the Romans.[4]

Private study, however, was an exceptional privilege, available only to those who were literate and who had disposable income. It is doubtful that those two prerequisites were ever widespread in the ancient world. Though Augustine had an advanced education and moderate means, there is no evidence that his mother, Monica, could read at all. Yet she moved easily in the scriptures, as her son demonstrated in his recollected dialogues of Cassiciacum. Augustine also recorded the probable reason for her knowledge, in a passage of the *Confessions* addressed to God in prayer: "[She] never

let a day go by unless she had brought an offering to your altar, and never failed to come to your church twice every day,
each morning and night, not to listen to empty tales and old
wives' gossip, but so that she might hear the preaching of
your word and you might listen to her prayers."[5] Monica's
profound Christian faith came "by hearing," and the hearing
took place twice a day in the church's liturgy.

Such liturgical proclamation—along with the corresponding component of liturgical hearing—appears as a constant
in biblical religion, from ancient Israel through the patristic
era and well beyond.[6]

⋘⋙

The covenant demanded such proclamation. M.G. Kline
speaks of "two standard elements" in the classic structure of
treaty-type covenants: one is witnesses, the other is "the direction for the depositing of the treaty text in the sanctuary for its
periodic reproclamation."[7] In God's covenant with mankind,
these elements take on cosmic proportions. Heaven and earth
are called upon as witnesses (see Dt 31:28 and 32:1), as is the
assembly itself (see Dt 31:19).

In the liturgy, the people assemble to hear the terms of
the law proclaimed, to bear witness to the oath, and to enact
and renew the covenant. It involves more than just the re-
publication of information—more than just "reading them
their rights." It is a dialogue. The people hear the word of
God and they respond in faith. Moses "took the book of the
covenant, and read it in the hearing of the people; and they

said, 'All that the Lord has spoken we will do, and we will be obedient' " (Ex 24:7). To put it in more familiar terms: the assembly hears the readings in every liturgy, and they respond with the creed and the anaphora—the oath and the offering of sacrifice.

Implicit in every element of the process—proclamation, hearing, and response—is the divine authority of God's word. All human covenants invoked God (or the gods) as witness. But the divine covenants were different, since in all of these God himself was involved, not merely as a witness and judge, but as a covenanting party. Men might violate their covenant oaths; but the "word of the Lord" stood as an ultimate and irrevocable authority—a divine speech act. "Let God be true though every man be false" (Rom 3:4).

The phrase "the word of the Lord" appears hundreds of times in the Hebrew scriptures. It is the authority that Moses invokes for his law and the prophets for their oracles. It is, according to the historical books, the authority behind the inspired deeds of the kings. The "word of the Lord" that reveals the covenant law is the very "word" by which God created the universe: "By the word of the Lord the heavens were made, and all their host by the breath of his mouth" (Ps 33:6). God's word, then, stands as objective truth, as immovable as a mountain, as unalterable as the moon and stars.

"By the breath of his mouth," God made the world and inspired the scriptures, according to the Psalm. The Pauline term for God's role in the authorship of scripture is *theopneustos,* literally "God-breathed." It appears in the second Letter to Timothy: "All scripture is inspired by God and profitable for teaching, for reproof, for correction, and for training in righteousness" (2 Tim 3:16). This passage—like all New Testament references to "scripture"—speaks, of course, of the Old Testament writings. For Jesus and his disciples, and indeed all his Jewish contemporaries, the scriptures held a unique authority. They were "living oracles" (Acts 7:38) "delivered by angels" (Acts 7:53). Cardinal Augustin Bea made a concise summary of the New Testament view of scriptural authority. It is worth quoting at length:

> *According to the New Testament, there exists a collection of writings which are called "Scripture" (see Jn 2:22; 10:35; Gal 3:8; 1 Pt 2:6; 2 Pt 1:20) or "the Scriptures" (Mt 21:42; 22:29; Jn 5:39; Ac 17:2, 11; 18:24; Rom 15:4), or the "Holy Scriptures" (Rom 1:2). This collection is considered by both Christ and the Apostles to be of divine origin and to it is attributed divine authority. With the words "it is written," Christ repeatedly appealed to the Scriptures as to an irrefutable authority (Mt 4:4–10; 22:31, 43; Jn 10:34–35). So did the Apostles (Ac 15:15–18; Rom 1:17).*
>
> *The divine origin of these Old Testament books is also implied by their being called simply "oracles of God" (Rom 3:2) or described as "prophetic" and their words as "prophecies" (cf. Mt 13:14; 15:7; Rom 16:26; 1 Pt 1:10; 2 Pt 1:19–20)—prophetic being the term used to describe a man who brings to other men the message, the word of God.*
>
> *Moreover, in a series of texts, Christ and the Apostles, referring to the Old Testament, affirm that God himself is*

*present in these writings because He himself speaks in them,
or because the human authors speak "in the Holy Spirit" or
are "inspired by the Holy Spirit" (cf. Ac 1:16–18;
2:30–31; Mt 22:31–32, 43; 2 Pt 1:19–21; 2 Tim
3:16–17). Hebrews introduces a quotation from Psalm 95
with the words: "the Holy Spirit says" (Heb 3:7; cf. 4:4–5;
9:8; 10:15). Moreover, in Matthew, quotations from the Old
Testament are introduced with the words: "All this took place
to fulfill what the Lord had spoken by the prophet. . . ." (Mt
1:22; cf. also 2:15). Because God was considered the Author
of Scripture, it was considered necessary and inevitable that
the Scripture should "be fulfilled" (cf. Mt 5:18–19; Lk
24:44; Ac 1:16 etc.).*[8]

The divine authority of scripture is implicit in the act of
liturgical proclamation;[9] but it is almost always made explicit
as well in the texts of the liturgy. The church traditionally
begins or ends the readings with an acclamation of their authority: "The word of the Lord!" Or, in the Byzantine tradition: "Wisdom! Be attentive!" The wisdom of God speaks
to his people.

The church publicly proclaims the scriptures in the
liturgy because they are the documents of the covenant,
which is solemnly renewed in the ritual worship of God's
people. The church requires only "canonical" texts to be
read in the liturgy, because only they set the terms of
the covenant in a divinely authoritative way. Only "The
word of the Lord" is appropriate for liturgical proclamation,
because only "The word of the Lord"—the word that cre-

ated the cosmos—can be a word that is "living and active" (Heb 4:12).

Scripture is, in this sense, profoundly sacramental. Augustine spoke of each of the church's sacraments as a "visible word" *(verbum visibile),* and of the word as an "audible sacrament" *(sacramentum audible).*[10] In the last generation, theologians such as Lucien Deiss and F. X. Durrwell described a "real presence" of Christ in the scriptures.[11] Aimé Georges Martimort made the necessary distinctions: "while the Word of God is not a sacrament in the strict sense, its proclamation in the liturgy has a special and unmatched authority and power. Moreover, it is the power exerted by this Word in the saving actions of Christ that founds the efficacy of the Church's sacramental actions."[12]

Scripture conveys the divine word, then, in a way that is analogous to sacramental efficacy. That is why the church has traditionally understood the scriptures to be without error. Yet "without error" does not adequately describe the extent of the Bible's sacramentality. Other books can be free of error—for example, a well-edited algebra textbook in its eighth edition—but no other book has God as its author, and so no other text conveys God's saving power so purely: "The words that I have spoken to you are spirit and life" (Jn 6:63).

Scripture's authority is thus an extension of Christ's own authority, and its characteristics are analogous to those of Christ himself. Jesus Christ is God's Word incarnate in humanity, without sin; the Bible is the word inspired, without error. Jesus Christ is fully human and fully divine; the scriptures are both fully divine and fully human, with the Holy

Spirit as their principal author and human writers as their instrumental authors. Scripture partakes of the mystery it imparts: that is, the mystery of Christ himself. In the words of Pope Pius XII: "For as the substantial Word of God became like to men in all things, 'except sin,' so the words of God, expressed in human language, are made like to human speech in every respect, except error."[13]

The Second Vatican Council described this relationship in its constitution *Dei Verbum* (chapter 11):

> *Those divinely revealed realities which are contained and presented in sacred scripture have been committed to writing under the inspiration of the Holy Spirit. For holy mother church, relying on the belief of the apostles (see Jn 20:31; 2 Tim 3:16; 2 Pt 1:19–20; 3:15–16), holds that the books of both the Old and New Testaments in their entirety, with all their pasts, are sacred and canonical because written under the inspiration of the Holy Spirit, they have God as their author and have been handed on as such to the church herself. In composing the sacred books, God chose men and while employed by him they made use of their powers and abilities, so that with him acting in them and through them, they, as true authors, consigned to writing everything and only those things which he wanted.*
>
> *Therefore, since everything asserted by the inspired authors or sacred writers must be held to be asserted by the Holy Spirit, it follows that the books of scripture must be acknowledged as teaching solidly, faithfully and without error*

*that truth which God, for the sake of our salvation, wished
to see confided in the sacred Scriptures.*[14]

Dei Verbum makes clear that inspiration is not merely for
the sake of an unerring text, but "for the sake of our salvation." Still, an unerring text "follows" logically from the
doctrine of inspiration. Divine authorship is an act of God
and, as such, it precludes error. The Second Vatican Council builds here upon the tradition of the fathers, summarized
in the encyclical *Providentissimus Deus* of Pope Leo XIII:
"For all the books which the church receives as sacred and
canonical are written wholly and entirely with all their parts,
at the dictation of the Holy Spirit; and so far is it from being
possible that any error can coexist with inspiration, that inspiration not only is essentially incompatible with error, but
excludes and rejects it as absolutely and necessarily as it is impossible that God himself, the supreme Truth, can utter that
which is not true. This is the ancient and unchanging faith of
the church."[15]

What Leo and Vatican II made explicit had been implicit
in Christian doctrine since the first generations. Clement of
Rome, writing perhaps as early as 69 A.D. (and certainly no
later than 96), assumed it in its fullness: "Look carefully into
the scriptures," he wrote, "which are the true utterances of
the Holy Spirit. Observe that nothing of an unjust or counterfeit character is written in them."[16] Clement's teaching
found further amplification in Justin, Irenaeus, Theophilus,
and Tatian.[17] In the works of the later fathers, we find the

most eloquent witness in the correspondence between the two great western exegetes of the fifth century; Augustine wrote to Jerome: "I confess to your charity that I have learned to defer this respect and honor to those scriptural books only which are now called canonical, that I believe most firmly that no one of those authors has erred in any respect in writing."[18]

The idea of scripture's divine authority exercised a profound influence on early Christian liturgy. The church venerated the sacred page because of its *sacramentality,* which was analogous to that of the eucharist. The first millennium of Christianity was characterized by a consistently high view of scriptural inspiration and a consistently high sacramentology. Word and sacrament commanded reverence both in doctrinal expression and in devotional life. The custom of kissing the book of gospels, which remains with the church today, arose in those early centuries, as did the custom of "enthroning" the biblical books in the church. "All the liturgies had the reading of the gospel preceded by a procession in which lights and incense were used to honor the book as a sign of Christ's presence."[19] Germanus of Constantinople taught: "the entrance of the gospel signified the coming of the Son of God."[20] From the patristic era onward, ecumenical councils were convened with the solemn enthronement of the scriptures, symbolizing Christ present with the assembled bishops, judging them and presiding over them.[21]

In third-century Egypt, Origen urged his listeners to adopt a very practical piety toward both scripture and eucharist: "You who are accustomed to attending the divine mysteries know how, when you receive the body of the Lord, you guard it with all care and reverence lest any small part should fall from it, lest any piece of the consecrated gift be lost. For you believe yourself guilty, and rightly so, if anything falls from there through your negligence. But if you are so careful to preserve his body, and rightly so, why do you think that there is less guilt to have neglected God's word than to have neglected his body?"[22]

In the fifth century, Paulinus of Nola demonstrated this reverence in the most concrete way. In a poem he described an Italian basilica, whose apse had two niches carved into its wall. In the first niche, the church reserved the sacrament of the altar; in the second niche were kept the scriptures.[23]

Dei Verbum summarized this tradition of reverence when it spoke, metaphorically, of the "table of the word" in addition to the table of the altar (n. 51).

Post-Reformation apologetics have sometimes reduced all discussion of the liturgy to a defense of transubstantiation. Catholic apologists emphasize the formula of consecration while relegating the scriptural readings to an almost incidental position. The classic experience was far different. Consider the confession made by Felix, a lector in Abitina, North Africa, in 304 A.D.: "We always convene at the Eucharist for the reading of the Lord's scriptures." Felix had been arrested, along with forty-odd others, during the celebration of Sunday Mass. Within days of making his confession, they died as martyrs for Christ in word and sacrament.[24]

The word is the Lord's, but it is revealed to mankind. It must be written, but primarily so that it can be proclaimed "in the midst of the assembly" (Sir 15:5) in every generation. Theologian Jeremy Driscoll said it with startling simplicity: "The book is a means to an end." And the end, he explained, is "the presence of the living Word in the midst of the believing assembly, accomplishing and extending to that assembly what has been accomplished in concrete historical events."[25] Put, by Driscoll, into even more lapidary terms: "Scripture is the *announcement* of the Word of God; liturgy is its *actualization.*"[26]

And the words of the gospel, like the Word they signify, do come with power. The liturgy itself attests to this. At the end of the gospel in every Mass, the rubrics instruct the priest or deacon to kiss the book, saying inaudibly, "May the words of the gospel wipe away our sins." It is the *words* of the gospel that bring about that saving effect.

"The book is a means to an end." Thus has it ever been. "And the Lord said to Moses, 'Write this as a memorial in a book and recite it in the ears of Joshua' " (Ex 17:14).

CHAPTER 6

THE PERSISTENCE OF MEMORY:
ANAMNESIS AND ACTUALIZATION

IN THE LITURGY read each Passover by devout Jews, there appears a quotation from Deuteronomy: "Remember the day when thou camest forth out of the land of Egypt all the days of thy life" (Dt 16:3). This is followed by reflections on the passage by the ancient sages, all of them assuming that commandment applied not only to the generation of the exodus, but to all Jews of all time. Every age, without exception, must "remember" the day of Israel's deliverance from Egypt. The Haggadah concludes with a moving interpretation: "Had it been written 'the days of thy life,' it would have meant this world only; 'all the days of thy life' means that the times of the Messiah are included as well."[1]

The Lord commanded Israel to observe the Passover as "a memorial day, and you shall keep it as a feast to the Lord; throughout your generations you shall observe it as an ordinance for ever" (Ex 12:14).

The "memorial" aspect of Passover is manifest throughout the Haggadah. The purpose of the feast is so that Israel might not forget the mighty deeds that God worked for the sake of their liberation from Egyptian bondage. Yet Passover is more than a mere "memorial"—more than just a commemoration of an historical event. For the Israelites, the Passover seder marked the renewal of their covenant with God. On that day, the covenant was extended in time. On that day they were renewed as God's people—his earthly family by covenant. To put it in terms of scholastic theology: the seder, like circumcision, possessed the power to effect what it signified. To borrow Austin's term once again, these rites constituted speech-acts, performative utterances.

To observe the Passover memorial was a defining character-istic of membership in God's covenant people, as remembrance was a defining characteristic of the covenant. Even "secular" covenants followed this pattern. In the ancient Near East, treaties between nations were sworn covenants, and they were usually ratified in a canonical document, which would later be opened and reproclaimed at predetermined intervals of time. The doc-ument customarily began with an historical prologue, which vividly described the exploits of the monarch (the suzerain) or his deputy who had made the covenant.[2] In secular covenants, reproclamation served several purposes. It reminded the cove-nanting parties of the blessings and curses attached to fulfillment or non-fulfillment of their obligations. Moreover, by recounting the past accomplishments of the suzerain, it reminded the subor-dinate (vassal) party of his prodigious ability to enforce the terms of the covenant. The historical prologue was at once an implied promise and an implied threat. Its public reading was a reminder, but it was more than that. It was a recommitment to the stated terms, and it renewed the people's commitment to the covenant for another year or another generation.

The divine covenant came with similar stipulations. The

law in Deuteronomy commands future monarchs to begin their reign with actions designed to engrave the covenant in memory: "And when he sits on the throne of his kingdom, he shall write for himself in a book a copy of this law, from that which is in the charge of the Levitical priests; and it shall be with him, and he shall read in it all the days of his life, that he may learn to fear the Lord his God, by keeping all the words of this law and these statutes, and doing them . . . so that he may continue long in his kingdom, he and his children, in Israel" (Dt 17:18–20).

Key to the keeping of a covenant was its remembrance; and the mnemonic key to remembrance was repetition. This was all the more true of the divine covenants recorded in the Bible. When the people gathered to establish or renew their covenant with God, they remembered his past deeds, which they held as a pledge of his future blessings. For the sake of remembrance, the people required certain institutions: canonical scriptures, a canonical liturgy—a tradition. The great first-century rabbi Gamaliel spoke of the seder in strictly rubrical terms: "Whosoever has not said [the biblical verses concerning] these three things at Passover has not fulfilled his obligation: Passover, unleavened bread, and bitter herbs: 'Passover'—because God passed over the houses of our fathers in Egypt; 'unleavened bread'—because our fathers were redeemed from Egypt; 'bitter herbs'—because the Egyptians embittered the lives of our fathers in Egypt."[3] The place of this remembrance is among a great nation, but a nation that is primarily a family—God's family, who share kinship with him by means of covenant. The Passover remembrance preserves this sense because it ordinarily takes place in a household, where the dialogue passes between father and son: "And when in time to come your son asks you, 'What does this mean?' you shall say to him, 'By strength of hand the Lord brought us out of Egypt, from the house of bondage' " (Ex 13:14).

The idea of remembrance is pervasive in biblical religion. The Old Testament renders it in the terms *zikkaron* and *askarah,* words that share a common Hebrew root. The New Testament (and the Septuagint translation of the Old Testament) uses the terms *anamnesis* and *mnemosynon,* which share a common Greek root. The Greek and Hebrew words are translated into English variously (and sometimes erratically) as "remembrance," "memorial," "memory," and "commemoration."

The inconsistency is understandable, as the ancient terms do present a difficulty for translators. For the concept conveyed by the original terms has no true equivalent in modern English—or indeed most modern languages. When Max Thurian wrote his two-volume study of *anamnesis* in the Old and New Testaments, he rejected the word "remembrance," and he noted that F. J. Leenhardt before him had dispensed with "memorial" as equally insufficient.[4]

We cannot translate these terms, and yet we must. For Christians find *anamnesis* prominent at a critical moment of salvation history. While instituting the eucharist as the rite of the new covenant, Jesus enjoined his disciples to "Do this in remembrance *[anamnesis]* of me" (Lk 22:19; 1 Cor 11:25). In the text itself, the new covenant, like the old, is bound up with a particular form of *anamnesis.*

What Jesus meant—and, in fact, what the rabbis meant—

by "remembrance" was not a simple act of memory or imagination. R. L. Wilken has perhaps best defined the term as to "recall by making present."[5] It is not merely a recollected thought, but a re-actualizing, a re-presenting, what Christian tradition calls a real presence.

Even in discussing the Jewish liturgy, however, Thurian did not hesitate to call this process "sacramental."

> *As they ate . . . the Jews could re-live mystically,* sacramentally, *the events of the deliverance and Exodus from Egypt. They became contemporaries of their forefathers and were saved with them. . . . The sacramental mystery belongs both to the Judaic and the Christian tradition and expresses the biblical meaning of the* salvation-history *which was accomplished in time* once for all *but which is equally* present *at all times by* Word *and* Sacrament. *. . . The Eucharist, instituted in this tradition and context, presents the same conception of the mystery of history, the mystery of salvation-history, present in the liturgical and sacramental action.*[6]

The events of biblical history are irrevocably past. They are not repeated. They are, however, repeatedly re-presented to believers in the liturgy, not in a merely theoretical or propositional way, but in a way that is real and actual. "What is the liturgy?" asked Blessed James Alberione. "It is the actualization of the Bible."[7]

Cyprian Vagaggini explained how the liturgy makes the events of salvation history immediate for the assembly and for the individual worshiper: "the liturgy in some way, *in sacra-*

mento, makes present the whole mystery of Christ, sacred history, realizing it in individual souls." Vagaggini continued:

> *historical passages . . . have not only the significance of a purely historical commemoration of the event, now past, to which they refer, but have also in the liturgical action the significance of a present application to each of the faithful of the value and redemptive fruit of that event. Thus the redemptive power of these events is in its own way newly actualized and prolonged because it is newly applied. Therefore, it can be said that these events, in the liturgy, are really re-actualized, not as historical events (as if, for example, the Mass of Christmas renewed the nativity of our Lord in the same way that every Mass renews, in its own way unbloodily, the sacrifice of Golgotha), but in their redemptive power.*[8]

The liturgy draws the believer into the drama of the divine economy, not as a spectator, but as a participant. The stream of salvation history cascades from generation to generation through the course of the divine liturgy. The participant in the Passover must speak of the exodus not in the third person, but in the first person: "It is because of that which the Lord did for me when I came forth out of Egypt" (Ex 13:8).[9] The Haggadah records a saying of the sages: "In every generation, a Jew is obligated to regard himself as if he personally had gone out of Egypt."[10] "Here," commented Thurian, "is that sacramental realism that emphasizes the actualization of the historical deliverance."[11]

We can recognize, in actualization, the continuing pattern of God's work in the divine economy. What the church discerns in history's typological pattern, believers experience in the sacraments. Cardinal Danielou's summary is as clear as it is complete:

> *The sacraments are conceived in relation to the acts of God in the Old Testament and the New. God acts in the world; His actions are the* mirabilia, *the deeds that are His alone. God creates, judges, makes a covenant, is present, makes holy, delivers. These same acts are carried out in the different phases of the history of salvation. There is, then, a fundamental analogy between these actions.* The sacraments are simply the continuation in the era of the Church of God's acts in the Old Testament and the New. *This is the proper significance of the relationship between the Bible and the liturgy. The Bible is a sacred history; the liturgy is a sacred history.*[12]

The typological pattern recorded in scripture has not passed away. The scriptures themselves conclude with the Book of Revelation, which applies typology to all subsequent history, until the end of time. Thus, the "memorial" or "remembrance" of liturgical celebrations involves not only a looking backward, but a looking forward as well. Sofia Cavalletti wrote: "The typological approach guides us to see each event in history as linked to what preceded it and at the same time projected toward the end—'when God will be all in all' (1 Cor 15:28). Only such a reading respects the weight of the divine mystery in history. In order to see this mystery in its richness, we must not neglect the eschatological expectation inherent in the Jewish and Christian approach to history."[13]

Liturgy, then, involves praise and thanksgiving for past and present events, and hopeful anticipation of future events. Wilken remarked, poetically: "Liturgy is always in the present tense. The past becomes a present presence that opens a new future."[14]

Critics outside the Christian tradition have faulted the use of typology as the church's wrongful appropriation of Israel's legacy. But many Jewish scholars have defended the legitimacy of this Christian exegetical tradition. Alan Segal, for example, wrote that "Israelite history . . . sees the past as a paradigm for the present. Past events are consciously used as liturgical models for the covenantal meaning of human destiny. . . . Isaiah declares that the events of the past are paradigms for the present and future."[15] For Jews as for Christians—all those who share the patrimony of Israel—past actions provide *liturgical* models for *covenantal* living. Segal concluded from this: "Although the Christian interpretation was new, this kind of reinterpretation of Scripture was a standard procedure during the period and was absolutely justifiable from the perspective of any contemporary. . . . In short, the reinterpretation of Scripture was normal for any group of the first century."[16]

This, then, has been a constant of biblical religion: the typological interpretation of history and its application to liturgy. We see it as much in the realism of Josephus as in the allegorizing of Philo. It is everywhere in the Christian fathers. Consider the glorious summary statement of Augustine, preached in preparation for the Easter Vigil Mass, circa 393 A.D.:

We firmly believe, brethren, that the Lord has died for our sins. . . . All of that happened once and for all, as you know well enough. And yet we have the liturgical solemnities which we celebrate as, during the course of the year, we come to the date of particular events. Between the truth of the events and the solemnities of the liturgy there is no contradiction, as if the latter were a lie. The historical truth is what happened once and for all, but the liturgy makes those events always new for the hearts that celebrate them with faith. The historical truth shows us the events just as they happened, but the liturgy, while not repeating them, celebrates them and prevents them from being forgotten. Thus, on the basis of historical truth, we say that Easter happened once only and will not happen again, but, on the basis of the liturgy, we can say that Easter happens every year. Thanks to the liturgy, the human mind reaches the truth and proclaims its faith in the Lord. [17]

The bond between scripture and liturgical worship, the use of typology in liturgy, these are characteristics shared by Jews and Christians, though with significant differences. Alexander Schmemann wrote: "Although in its outward forms this independent Christian worship clearly derives from specifically Hebrew 'prototypes,' no one would deny its newness in relation to the cult of the Temple and the synagogue. . . . Christians did not simply continue to take part in a cult which had become unnecessary and outmoded for them, they kept this cult as their own, in exactly the same way as when they read the Old Testament they understood it as Scripture about Christ." [18]

The *Catechism of the Catholic Church* urges believers to

learn from the similarities even as they are respectful of the distinctive marks of each: "The relationship between Jewish liturgy and Christian liturgy, but also their differences in content, is particularly evident in the great feasts of the liturgical year, such as Passover. Christians and Jews both celebrate the Passover. For Jews, it is the Passover of history, tending toward the future; for Christians, it is the Passover fulfilled in the death and Resurrection of Christ, though always in expectation of its definitive consummation" (CCC, n. 1096).

⁂

The liturgical memorial is always multifaceted. The people call to mind the covenant; they call to mind the glorious deeds of the God of the covenant; they remind God of the covenant. All of the memorial is for the glory of God; but all of the memorial is for the sake of mankind. God, after all, does not "need" worship from mankind; God stands in need of nothing. Nor, moreover, does God need to be "reminded" of anything; God is omniscient, and he is eternal, and so all time is constantly present to him. It is a mark of his saving condescension that he "remembers" his covenant with Abraham in order to complete the exodus of Abraham's descendants.

God, however, does not need remembrance. It is, rather, mankind that requires regular mementos of the covenant. Thus, liturgical worship rises to God's glory, but redounds always to the benefit of those who offer fitting worship. It is they who remember the covenant, and so renew the bond of kinship, and so remain within the covenant family.

Consider Moses' "memorial" to God in Exodus 32. The Israelites had just sinned grievously by their idolatrous worship of the golden calf. By this, they had merited death. Moses, however, intervenes on their behalf, invoking the memory of God's covenant with the patriarchs: "Remember Abraham, Isaac, and Israel, thy servants, to whom thou didst swear by thine own self, and didst say to them, 'I will multiply your descendants as the stars of heaven, and all this land that I have promised I will give to your descendants, and they shall inherit it for ever' " (Ex 32:13).

Moses' "memorial" is a typological foreshadowing of the remembrance of the new covenant. Moses himself stood as a Christlike mediator between God and Israel. Thurian observed: "It is the same intercession that the Church makes in the Eucharist, when it presents to God the crucified Christ."[19] For God's glory and the assembly's benefit, the church makes its remembrance as Moses made his. Indeed, Moses' litany of the patriarchal covenants finds echo in many of the church's historic liturgies, including the Roman Canon and the contemporary Eucharistic Prayer IV.

Covenant liturgy recalls past acts of deliverance. Covenant liturgy recalls sworn promises for future blessing. Thus, in Thurian's words: "The past deliverance becomes a pledge of that which is to come, which will be perfect and definitive."[20]

⚜

Yet fulfillment begins even now, in the Bible's actualization through the sacramental liturgy. The assurance of this rests upon scripture's divine inspiration, sacramentality, and canonicity. Christian worship can be life-transforming because the biblical word proclaimed is "not a human word but . . . truly is the word of God" (1 Thess 2:13). The transformation it effects is not merely psychological or motivational, but metaphysical. Again, the effectiveness of scripture does not depend on its motivational power; some passages, and even entire books of the Bible, may be opaque, dull, or shocking. Yet they possess more power than even the most exalted poetry. Poetry, to quote Auden, "makes nothing happen."[21]

God's word, on the other hand, when it is proclaimed in the liturgy, establishes the kingdom of heaven on earth. It constitutes the kingdom of heaven on earth. And it reveals the kingdom of heaven on earth. Alexander Schmemann noted: "The remembrance of Christ which He instituted (This do in remembrance of Me) is the affirmation of His 'Parousia,' of His presence; it is the actualization of His Kingdom."[22] This is what the sacraments signify, and this is what they effect in the church's life and in the lives of believers.

Ordinary human language, no matter how beautiful or persuasive, cannot do this. Only the sacred speech of God can perform the divine action of transforming bread and wine into the body and blood of God incarnate. Only the sacred speech of God can bring man into communion with the divine. The liturgical proclamation is nothing less than a theophany, a divine manifestation of Christ the King.

The Pontifical Biblical Commission made this point forcefully in its 1993 document *The Interpretation of the Bible in the Church*: "it is above all through the liturgy that Christians come into contact with scripture. . . . In principle, the liturgy, and especially the sacramental liturgy, the high point of which is the eucharistic celebration, brings about the most perfect actualization of the biblical texts. . . . Christ is then 'present in his word, because it is he himself who speaks when sacred scripture is read in the Church' *(Sacrosanctum Concilium 7)*. Written text thus becomes living word."[23]

In God's plan of salvation, the Bible leads God's people to the liturgy. In the liturgy, the written text of scripture becomes the living word of God. The Bible's meaning and purpose are fulfilled in the liturgy—the words of scripture become "spirit and life . . . the words of eternal life" (Jn 6:63, 68).

To return for a moment to the story that began this book: Was Anthony of Egypt convinced by the reason of the argument he heard in the story of the rich young man? That is unlikely; the gospel presents an elliptical argument at best. The divine word, however, filled in the ellipses and, by the power of the Spirit, moved Anthony to hear this story as the story of the everlasting covenant, and to hear the Lord speaking directly to Anthony himself. "For in the sacred books, the Father who is in heaven meets his children with great love and speaks with them" *(Dei Verbum 22)*. When the Father speaks, as he did in creation, worlds come into being, lives are changed. Only the word of God, living and active in the liturgy, possesses the power to cut to the heart.

Pope John Paul II, in his apostolic letter *Rosarium Maria Virginis,* provided a brief but authoritative account of the process of the liturgical actualization of the word of God:

We need to understand this . . . biblical sense of remembrance (zakar) as a making present of the works brought about by God in the history of salvation. The Bible is an account of saving events culminating in Christ himself. These events not only belong to "yesterday"; they are also part of the "today" of salvation [emphasis mine]. This making present comes about above all in the liturgy: what God accomplished centuries ago did not only affect the direct witnesses of those events; it continues to affect people in every age with its gift of grace.[24]

❧❦❧

Liturgical *anamnesis* brought the life of Anthony of Egypt into the great stream of salvation history. The typological pattern, evident throughout the divine economy, now worked actively and fruitfully in the life of Anthony as he corresponded more perfectly to the will of God, giving himself completely to the contemplative life. That is actualization at its purest.

Cavalletti explored the profound relationships between liturgical *anamnesis*, typology, and the lives of believers:

Memorial and typology each annul the distance between historical events, causing them to converge into the "eternal present" of a manifestation of salvation. . . . Typology makes the listening to the Word today capable of creating a link with past history and what is still the object of hope. . . . The memorial makes it possible to live today the salvation already realized in the events of the past and projected towards the eschatological completion, awaited now in hope and prayer.[25]

Christian history recounts the story, time and again, in seemingly infinite variety, yet always according to the pattern. Robin Darling Young, in an important study, noted that the stories of the earliest martyrs often depict their martyrdom as a "public liturgy." The authors dramatize the sacrifice of persecuted Christians as an extension of the eucharistic sacrifice.[26] Sometimes the martyrs themselves used this unself-conscious technique—as when Ignatius expressed his wish to be ground like wheat in the teeth of the lions,[27] or when Polycarp prayed in the form of a eucharistic prayer at his execution, and his burning body gave off the aroma of baking bread.[28]

Sometimes, the reality appeared in the courtroom records, as in Abitina, where the convicted Christians greeted their death sentence with liturgical acclamations: *Deo gratias!*

Martyrdom is an actualization, again, in its purest form: an imitation of Christ that is a true communion with Christ, a willing participation in his life and death—his complete self-giving. This we find everywhere in the lives of the "canonized" saints. For the martyr, the monk, and every baptized Christian must make a perfect offering of all of life, to the moment of death. Like the old law, though in a new way, the new law extends the reach of the sacrificial liturgy to every hour, waking and sleeping, spent in the kitchen, bedroom, boardroom, assembly line, or hospital bed.

In Christian lives, the scriptures are actualized, and that is how the kingdom comes to earth. Actualization is infinitely more than a private act of piety. It is transformative, not just of the believer, but of the world.

CHAPTER 7

Proclamation and *Parousia*

IF THERE IS a pattern to be found in actualization through martyrdom, we might find its roots in the scriptural acts of the protomartyr Stephen (Acts 6–7). Stephen's deeds served as models for persecuted Christians in the next centuries, and Luke's account surely served as a model for future biographers of the saints.

What pattern do we find in Luke's narrative? Brought before the high priest, the elders, and the scribes, Stephen testifies at length, in what amounts to a sermon sketching the works of the divine economy since the time of Abraham. He highlights the covenants and shows the typological fulfillment of all previous history in the death of Jesus Christ. Then, at the climax of Stephen's impromptu trial comes what appears to be a supernatural interruption of the natural course of events.

Stephen, "full of the Holy Spirit, gazed into heaven and saw the glory of God, and Jesus standing at the right hand of God; and he said, 'Behold, I see the heavens opened, and the son of man standing at the right hand of God' " (Acts 7:55–56).

Stephen, an ordained deacon in the nascent church, had proclaimed the word of the Lord. His public proclamation then culminated in the *parousia* of Jesus. Like John the Seer, who wrote while "in the Spirit on the Lord's day" (Rev 1:10), Stephen is "full of the Holy Spirit" at the moment of his apocalyptic vision. This remarkable event led to Stephen's sacrificial self-offering (7:59) and his last words, which echo those of Jesus on the cross (Acts 7:60; cf. Lk 23:34).

Stephen's testimony and self-offering surely influenced later martyrs such as Ignatius and Polycarp, men of the next generation whose way to martyrdom involved both public proclamation and voluntary sacrifice. But, apart from any extraordinary mystical gifts, did these men also share his experience of the *parousia* of the son of man?

For many people today, the difficulty in addressing that question will be an accurate understanding of the term *parousia*.

❧❧

Christians have always used the word *parousia* to denote the coming of Christ, with all its attendant events, such as the judgment, the end of the world, and the renewal of the world. The word has become problematic in recent generations, however, because it evokes an ever-growing complex of associations, even among scholars. Some of these associated ideas have their origin in antiquity; others are of a more recent vintage: for example, from the millennialist controversies of the ninth or the nineteenth centuries. For our purposes, it will be helpful to study the first-century usage of the word.

The Greek word *parousia* means, literally, "presence, coming, arrival, or advent." In popular Christian parlance, it has come to mean, specifically, Christ's return in glory at the end of time. Jesus himself used the term many times in describing that eschatological event. For example: "as the lightning comes from the east and shines as far as the west, so will be the coming *[parousia]* of the Son of man" (Mt 24:27).

Because of such passages, it can be difficult for us to think of *parousia* as meaning anything but a "coming in glory"—a dramatic divine interruption of history. But that is a theological projection onto a fairly common, and even mundane, Greek word. "Coming in glory" was not the meaning of the word in its original usage. *Parousia* could describe the visit of an emperor or king, and it was sometimes used that way. It could also describe a much less impressive event. When St. Paul, for example, speaks of his own *parousia,* he gives it a decidedly self-deprecating cast: "For they [Paul's critics] say, 'His letters are weighty and strong, but his bodily presence *[parousia]* is weak, and his speech of no account' " (2 Cor 10:10). Note that, here, all Paul means by his own *parousia* is his "bodily presence," which he insists is unimpressive to the senses. He uses the word in the same sense in his letter to the Philippians: "Therefore, my beloved, as you have always obeyed, so now, not only as in my presence *[parousia]* but much more in my absence, work out your own salvation with fear and trembling" (Phil 2:12). In both passages, Paul uses *parousia* to mean an immediate bodily presence, a presence that is real, though visually and aurally unimposing.

It is surely possible, and even probable, that Jesus used the word *parousia* to connote the same things—to mean a bodily presence that was real, but unimposing to the senses.

I acknowledge that this is not the interpretation of *parousia* given by some modern interpreters, especially among fundamentalists. But we would do well to consider the expectations of Jesus' own generation. The Jews of his time read the Old Testament prophecies as predictions of a messiah who would come with military power, overwhelming his enemies with spectacular victories. They were not prepared for a carpenter who laid down his life as a victim. Jesus had promised repeatedly that the kingdom was coming without delay. Midway through the "little apocalypse" of Matthew's gospel, Jesus says: "Truly, I say to you, this generation will not pass away till all these things take place" (Mt 24:35). Those utterances were canonized as scripture and read in the liturgy, without hesitation or interruption, even as Jesus' own generation receded into history.

None of this precludes a *parousia* of Christ at the end of history. Theologians call that "coming" of Christ the "final advent" or "plenary *parousia*"—not because Christ will have a greater fullness then, but rather because humankind will be able to behold him in his fullness, with senses unveiled. "Beloved, we are God's children now; it does not yet appear what we shall be, but we know that when he appears we shall be like him, for we shall see him as he is" (1 Jn 3:2).

Since Christ's coming, he is present in the world in a way

that he was not in the old covenant; yet he remains veiled in a way that he will not be veiled at the consummation of history. In its interpretation of the phrase "Thy kingdom come," the *Catechism of the Catholic Church* states: "The Kingdom of God has been coming since the Last Supper and, in the Eucharist, it is in our midst. The kingdom will come in glory when Christ hands it over to his Father" (n. 2816).[1]

In his incarnation, Jesus came; and, as he passed from human sight, he promised to sustain his presence forever: "I am with you always, to the close of the age" (Mt 28:20). Thus, his *parousia*—his presence—remained with Christians, even as they prayed for its plenitude.

◦✿◦

Several generations of scholars, from the nineteenth to the mid-twentieth century, told the story of the primitive church in terms of eschatological expectation and eventual disappointment, followed by ecclesiastical damage control. Jesus predicted a glorious return, which the first believers died awaiting. In the words of Alfred Loisy: Christ preached the kingdom, but left only the church.[2] In this view, Stephen's vision represented an ecclesiastical effort to reinterpret Jesus' eschatology, recasting it as a "realized eschatology"—a spiritualizing of a formerly material expectation.

Jaroslav Pelikan wrote forcefully against such scholars, who find a supposedly "catastrophic" sense of delay in the early texts: "Any such description is based on too simplistic a view of the role of apocalyptic in the teaching of Jesus and in the early church. Nor is it corroborated by later texts, for one looks in vain for proof of a bitter disappointment over the postponement of the parousia or of a shattering of the early Christian communities by the delay of the Lord's return."[3]

The "catastrophic" interpretation has grown increasingly untenable with the documentary discoveries of the past hundred and fifty years. Subsequent scholarship has demonstrated persuasively that realized eschatology represents the most primitive strain of Christian eschatology—and that Christian hope for an imminent *parousia* was actually born of faith in a liturgical *parousia*. Pelikan marshaled the ancient literary and liturgical evidence and summarized the argument in a conclusive way:

> *That impression is corroborated by the references to the "coming" of Christ in the scraps of early liturgies that have come down to us. For example, the Benedictus of Matthew 21:9 was clearly an affirmation of the coming of the end with the promised arrival of the messianic kingdom. But at least as early as the Apostolic Constitutions, and presumably earlier, the liturgical practice of the church employed these same words to salute either the celebrant or the eucharistic presence. . . . The coming of Christ was "already" and "not yet": he had come already—in the incarnation, and on the basis of the incarnation would come in the Eucharist; he had come already in the Eucharist, and would come at the last in the new cup that he would drink with them in his Father's kingdom. When the ancient liturgy prayed, "Let grace*

come [or "Let the Lord come"], and let the world pass away," its eschatological perspective took in both the final coming of Christ and his coming in the Eucharist. The eucharistic liturgy was not a compensation for the postponement of the parousia, but a way of celebrating the presence of one who had promised to return.[4]

Gregory Dix confirmed that this was not a later eschatology imposed on the primitive *kerygma*. Indeed, it was everywhere in the ancient *kerygma*. Dix maintained that this notion of a liturgical *parousia* was "universal" by the third century, and probably long before, since, he added, there are no exceptions to this rule: "no pre-Nicene author Eastern or Western whose eucharistic doctrine is at all fully stated" holds a different view.[5]

Consider just two examples from the ancient liturgies. The West Syrian Liturgy of St. James announces: "Let all mortal flesh be silent, and stand with fear and trembling, and meditate nothing earthly within itself: for the King of kings and Lord of lords, Christ our God, comes forward."[6] In its oldest Greek recensions, James consistently uses the word *parousia* to describe the liturgical theophany.[7] The Egyptian liturgy of Sarapion proclaims: "This sacrifice is full of your glory."[8] Similar passages can be found in the liturgies of Mark, Hippolytus, the Apostolic Constitutions, John Chrysostom, and Cyril of Alexandria, as well as the Roman Canon.[9]

What the ancients saw in the liturgy was the coming of

Christ: the *parousia*; and what they meant by *parousia* is what Catholic theology came to express as the "real presence" or "substantial presence" of Jesus Christ.[10]

In the liturgy—in the event that the Acts of the Apostles calls "the breaking of the bread and the prayers"—the earliest Christians experienced the glorious coming of the Lord, though there they could see him only with eyes of faith, recognizing him, as did the disciples at Emmaus, "in the breaking of the bread."

The earliest Christian vision was of Christ ascended as the heavenly high priest, offering a liturgy of praise that somehow resembled the liturgy of God's people on earth. Alan Segal observed that this notion—of a mediating priest at the right hand of God—was a motif common in Hellenistic and mystical Judaism as well. Both Jews and Christians interpreted Psalm 110 as a prophecy of the messiah who would rule as king and officiate as "a priest forever after the order of Melchizedek" (Ps 110:4). Segal found confirmation of this priestly ascension motif in the Letter to the Hebrews, which quotes Psalm 110:4 and comments: "he entered once for all into the Holy Place" (Heb 9:12).[11]

The earliest Christian vision, then, bore striking similarities to the apocalyptic vision of Stephen. Christ the eternal priest stood, like Stephen's "son of man," at God's right hand, fulfilling the liturgy of the ancient temple and officiating at the liturgy of the church. This is not a novelty with Christianity, but rather a profound development of the ancient Israel's understanding of divine worship.

The people of Israel considered their earthly liturgy to be a divinely inspired imitation of heavenly worship. Both Moses and Solomon constructed God's earthly dwellings—the tabernacle and the temple—according to a heavenly archetype revealed by God himself (see Ex 25–27; 1 Chr 28; Wis 9:8). The prophets expressed this belief in a mystical way, as they depicted the angels worshiping amid songs and trappings that were clearly recognizable from the Jerusalem temple (see Is 6 and Ezek 1). The hymns sung by the angels were the same songs the Levites sang before the earthly sanctuary.

We find the idea in full flower at the time of Jesus Christ and expressed in the non-canonical books of Enoch and Jubilees and in the Dead Sea Scrolls. What the priests did in the temple sanctuary was an earthly imitation of what the angels did in heaven.

None of this was mere pageantry. Both the heavenly and earthly liturgies had more than a ceremonial purpose. The angelic liturgy preserved a certain order not only in the courts of the Almighty, but in the entire universe. God had given over the governance of creation to his angels, and so the world itself was caught up in a cosmic liturgy: "Holy, holy, holy is the Lord of hosts; the whole earth is full of His glory" (Is 6:3). As Israel's priests performed their temple liturgy, they—like their counterparts in heaven—preserved and sanctified the order of the cosmos.

Thus, Israel's worship overflowed to form Israel's culture.

This is what made David a man after God's own heart. He wanted to configure earthly space and time so that all of the kingdom's temporal works flowed from worship and returned to God as a sacrifice of praise and thanksgiving. He moved the ark of the covenant to rest as the center of his capital city, and he planned a magnificent temple as its home. He endowed the priests and their attendants richly, and he himself composed beautiful liturgies for their use.

With all of that in their cultural and historical background, the Jews of Jesus' time would have recognized the beauty of his petition in the Lord's Prayer "Thy will be done on earth as it is in heaven," in a way that many of us today do not.

To the ancient People of God, heaven and earth were distinct, but earth traced the motions of heaven most clearly in the rites of the temple. They recognized that to worship God in this way was an awesome gift. Yet it was still only a shadow of the angels' worship—and only a shadow of the earthly worship that would be inaugurated by Jesus Christ.

By assuming human flesh, however, Christians believed that Jesus brought heaven to earth. Moreover, with his very flesh, he had fulfilled and perfected the worship of ancient Israel. No longer must the covenant-people worship in imitation of angels. In the liturgy of the new covenant, the renewed Israel—the church—worshiped *together with the angels*. Martimort explained: "This singular interplay of earth and heaven is characteristic of the Christian liturgy. There are not two liturgies, any more than there are two Churches. Rather, as the same Church is a pilgrim on earth and triumphant in heaven, so the same liturgy is celebrated here below in figurative rites and without figures 'beyond the veil' in the heavenly sanctuary."[12]

In the New Testament, the Book of Revelation revealed the *shared* liturgy of heaven and earth. Around the throne of God, men and angels bowed down and worshiped together (see Rev 5:14); an angel lifted the Seer up to stand beside him (Rev 19:10). Moreover, the renewed Israel—the Christian church—was portrayed as a kingdom of priests (Rev 1:6; 5:10; 20:6), so that all were admitted to the holiest inner sanctum of the temple.

The Book of Revelation, most especially, highlights the historical and cosmological development that has taken place. Erik Peterson explained: "We see clearly that the earthly Jerusalem with its temple worship has been the starting point for these ideas and images of primitive Christian literature; but the starting point has been left behind and it is no longer upon earth that Jerusalem is sought as a political power or centre of worship but in heaven, whither the eyes of all Christians are turned."[13]

Rabbi Baruch Levine, in his commentary on Leviticus, has noted the Mass's continuity with the worship of Jerusalem's temple. After the destruction of the temple in 70 A.D., rabbinic Judaism continued with non-sacrificial worship in the synagogue; Christianity's liturgy took up the temple's sacrificial liturgy, in a renewed form. "Christian worship in the form of the traditional mass affords the devout an experience of sacrifice, of communion, and proclaims that God is present. The Christian church, then, is a temple."[14]

The tradition of the old covenant's priesthood passed into the new covenant's priesthood. In the verse that immediately precedes Stephen's story in Acts, we learn that "a great many of the [temple] priests were obedient to the faith" (Acts 6:7). The fathers understood this liturgical and sacrificial connection between the temple and the church. Eusebius tells us that John "wore the sacerdotal plate," the *petalon,* until the end of his days, as did James of Jerusalem.[15] And the earliest Christian documents (*Didache,* Ignatius, Justin) agree in using overwhelmingly sacrificial language (sacrifice, altar, oblation) to describe the church's liturgy.[16]

In the worship of the new covenant, however, Christ himself now served as high priest of the liturgy in heaven and on earth—a liturgy led in the church by his clergy, who "preside in the place of God."[17] And Christians not only imitated the angels, but actively participated in the angelic worship. The sense of angelic presence is especially acute in the primitive liturgies.[18]

The early Christians professed their belief in the angelic presence and power in the heavenly liturgy, the church's liturgy, and the "cosmic liturgy" of all creation. God had delegated both liturgical and cosmic ministries to the angels; but Christians now shared that liturgical and cosmic authority as they worshiped with the angels. Thus, the Book of Revelation shows liturgical action as directing human history. At the onset of wars and bloodshed, we see "the wine of

God's wrath, poured unmixed into the cup of his anger" (Rev 14:10).

The doctrine of the angels, like the arm of God, has not been shortened over time; and it remains integral to every liturgy of the apostolic churches. In the Roman liturgy's prefaces, this theme is especially strong: "And so with all the choirs of angels in heaven, we proclaim your glory and join in their unending hymn of praise. . . . Holy, Holy, Holy . . ."

Cardinal Ratzinger has noted that the New Testament's apocalyptic imagery is overwhelmingly liturgical, and the church's liturgical language is overwhelmingly apocalyptic. "The *parousia* is the highest intensification and fulfillment of the liturgy," he writes. "And the liturgy is *parousia.* . . . Every Eucharist is *parousia,* the Lord's coming, and yet the Eucharist is even more truly the tensed yearning that He would reveal His hidden Glory"[19]

The patristic era provides no more stunning, and extensive, presentation of the heavenly-earthly liturgy than the theological meditation found in the fourth-century Syriac *Liber Graduum,* or Book of Steps:

> *Since we know that the body becomes a hidden temple and the heart a hidden altar for spiritual worship, let us be diligent in this public altar and before this public temple. . . . For our Lord and his first and last preachers did not erect in vain the church and the altar and baptism, all of which are visible to physical eyes. It is through these visible things, however, that we shall be in these heavenly things, which are invisible to eyes of flesh, our bodies becoming temples and*

our hearts altars (Heb 11:3). Let us open [the door] and enter into this visible church with its priesthood and its worship. . . . Then . . . that heavenly church and spiritual altar will be revealed to us and we will sacrifice praise upon it through the prayer of our hearts and the supplication of our bodies while believing in this visible altar and this priesthood, which serves [the altar] true for us.[20]

꧁꧂

The eucharist is the *parousia*. In the divine liturgy, Christ descends to the altar, and the assembly ascends to heaven with Christ. Heaven and earth, full of God's glory, unite in worship. What, then, of the other events customarily associated with the *parousia*? What of judgment? Whenever the New Testament speaks of Christ's coming, it speaks also of his judgment.

The eucharistic *parousia* is a real presence—and thus it is, necessarily, Christ coming in power to judge. His power is evident in its effects on those who receive communion. In his first Letter to the Corinthians, Paul speaks specifically of those who receive unworthily and so bring judgment upon themselves. "That is why many of you are weak and ill, and some have died" (11:30). For such unrepentant sinners, the eucharist is the final coming of Christ; it is the last judgment, and they are experiencing the curses stipulated in the covenant. A little over a generation later, Ignatius will put the doctrine in starkest terms: "Those, then, who speak against this gift of God, incur death."[21]

There is, however, an unspoken corollary to Paul's account of the judgment of sinners. With the eucharistic *parousia* comes also the judgment of the saints. If Christ's coming means sickness and death to sinners, how much more will his coming mean blessings and health to those who "discern the Lord's body"? A liturgy of ancient Egypt expresses this well at the very moment of consecration, when it asks God to make every communicant worthy "to receive a medicine of life for the healing of every sickness and . . . not for condemnation."[22] This echoes the still older praise of Ignatius of Antioch, who called the eucharist the "medicine of immortality, the antidote against death."[23]

It is the glorified Christ who comes in the eucharist, for communion with those who are worthy to receive the gift. For the saints, the judgment of the *parousia* is everlasting life, a share in Christ's own resurrected flesh. At the end of the second century, Irenaeus could ask: "how can they say that the flesh, which is nourished with the body of the Lord and with his blood, goes to corruption? . . . For the bread, which is produced from the earth, is no longer common bread, once it has received the invocation of God; it is then the eucharist, consisting of two realities, earthly and heavenly. So also our bodies, when they receive the eucharist, are no longer corruptible, but have the hope of the resurrection to eternity."[24]

And what of the kingdom that the early Christians so earnestly expected to come with the *parousia*—the kingdom that Christ himself had promised? After all, it was Jesus who set such a high level of expectation in the church; and it was

Jesus who pointed to its imminent fulfillment. Indeed, it was Jesus who established the eucharist as an eschatological event—a *parousia*—a coming of the King and the kingdom. We must not miss the small but significant details in the scriptural accounts of the Last Supper. As Jesus took the bread and wine, he said to his apostles: "I have earnestly desired to eat this passover with you before I suffer; for I tell you I shall not eat it until it is fulfilled in the kingdom of God. . . . I shall not drink of the fruit of the vine until the kingdom of God comes" (Lk 22:15–16, 18). As he instituted the sacrament, he instituted the kingdom. A moment later, he spoke of the kingdom in terms of a "table" (v. 27) and a "banquet" (v. 30)—language that will recur in the final chapters of the Book of Revelation. If we are looking for familiar apocalyptic language, we will find it aplenty in Luke's account of the Last Supper, but we will find it always expressed in eucharistic terms. Jesus goes on to speak of apocalyptic trials, in which believers are "sifted like wheat" (v. 31), language that will be taken up, in turn, by the martyrs Ignatius and Polycarp.

The kingdom indeed came, as Jesus had promised, within the generation of the disciples. The kingdom came as the church, which is constituted by the eucharist. The church's glory, like Christ's own glory, is not visible to bodily eyes. It is, in fact, obscured by the imperfections of its members. But recall that Christ compared the kingdom to a dragnet filled with fish and with trash; recall that he compared it to a field planted with both weeds and wheat. He could not have been speaking of the fulfillment of the kingdom at the end of time; for then there will be no mourning, no crying, no pain, nor anything accursed (see Rev 21:4, 22:3). He was speaking about the church that the first Christians knew—the church that is the kingdom.

The *Catechism* returns to this idea repeatedly: "The Church knows that the Lord comes even now in his Eucharist and that he is there in our midst. However, his presence is veiled. Therefore we celebrate the Eucharist 'awaiting the blessed hope and the coming of our Savior, Jesus Christ. . . .' " (n. 1404; see also n. 2816).

❧❧❧

Catholic theology since the Protestant Reformation has, understandably, emphasized the real presence of Christ in the eucharistic elements, under the appearance of bread and wine. That doctrine, after all, was the object of attacks by Calvin, Luther, and Zwingli.

But the Second Vatican Council moved the church beyond timely apologetics, and spoke of the timeless truth of Christ's presence in the Mass. The constitution *Sacrosanctum Concilium* pointed out three modes of Christ's presence in the Mass. He is especially present, said the council fathers, in the eucharistic species; but he is also present in the person of the officiating priest. Finally, "he is present in his word, since it is he himself who speaks when the holy scriptures are read in the church."[25]

Again, this is not a new idea. In the years before the council, Pierre Jounel wrote of the liturgical reading of the gospel as "in fact, a theophany, an appearance of Christ the King, the Son of God, of one substance with the Father, in the midst of the assembly."[26] Josef Jungmann agreed: "It is neither accidental nor fortuitous that when the Gospel has been read at Mass we greet the Lord as though present: *Gloria tibi, Domine!*"[27]

And the idea has strong patristic precedents. As I pointed out in an earlier chapter, the fathers often compared the reception of the word with the reception of the eucharist. Origen wrote: "We are said to drink the blood of Christ not only when we receive it according to the rite of the mysteries, but also when we receive his words, in which life dwells, as he said himself: 'The words that I have spoken to you are spirit and life.' "[28]

As in the "public liturgy" of Stephen's martyrdom, the church's proclamation culminated in *parousia* and then sacrifical self-offering and communion. "It is consummated" (Jn 19:30); and yet all members of the church still "wait in joyful hope for the coming of our savior Jesus Christ."

Inasmuch as . . . Christians are still living in this world, they expect, they wait for, this "parousia," they pray and keep the vigil for they do not know when the Son of Man shall come. And this expectation is expressed therefore in a new fasting, in a new state of awaiting.

This expectation, this yearning, is now constantly fulfilled and answered in the sacrament of the Lord's Presence, in the Eucharistic banquet.[29]

CHAPTER 8

WHERE TRADITION LIVES

As the Italians like to say, every translation is a traitorous act *(traditore* = traitor; *tradutore* = translator).* When we attempt to translate an ancient term like *anamnesis* into modern English, we inevitably forfeit a wealth of its meaning. We settle for *memory, recollection, recall, remembrance*—all of which suggest a fleeting psychological phenomenon. We must then spend chapters explaining that liturgical *anamnesis* is an action of real participation in actions past and future. It involves, but is not reducible to, a remembrance of things past. It is indeed an extension of ancient Israel's passover to believers today, but it is also a present act of worship and praise; and it is an anticipation of the heavenly liturgy that Christians hope to enjoy forever. Again, *anamnesis* is not merely a psychological act. The *anticipation* is a real *participation* in the heavenly liturgy, right here and right now. It is not wishful thinking; it is a true foretaste.

We encounter similar problems when we begin to speak of *tradition*—in Latin, *traditio*; in Greek, *paradosis*. To the modern mind, the word suggests an accumulation of inherited customs and lore. A vivid popular expression of this is the song "Tradition" sung by Tevye in the movie *Fiddler on the Roof.* For Tevye and for all the people of his village, tradition means a rich heritage of gender roles, societal duties, patterns of work, and rubrics for worship. Another familiar notion is that of rabbinic Judaism, where tradition is embodied in the voluminous record of the ancient rabbis' interpretation of the Torah, transmitted orally for generations before being set down in writing.

The church's living tradition includes all of these things,[1] but is not reducible to them, any more than *anamnesis* is reducible to mere memorial, or typology is reducible to literary symbolism. Tradition is divine revelation in its transmission through time. Tradition is one of the two distinct modes of the transmission of the gospel of Jesus Christ (scripture being the other mode). Both scripture and tradition flow "from the same divine wellspring, come together in some fashion to form one thing and move towards the same goal," according to the Second Vatican Council.[2] Basil the Great gave this doctrine its classic formulation when he made the distinction between apostolic *dogma* and apostolic *kerygma.* *Kerygma* represents the beliefs and practices that the apostles committed to writing, in the books eventually canonized as the New Testament. *Dogma* represents those teachings that have been passed on "in a mystery" by tradition. "In relation to true religion," Basil wrote, "both of these have the same force."[3]

The Second Vatican Council, in *Dei Verbum,* article 9, echoed Basil and elaborated on his teaching:

Sacred Scripture is the word of God inasmuch as it is consigned to writing under the inspiration of the divine Spirit, while sacred tradition takes the word of God entrusted by Christ the Lord and the Holy Spirit to the Apostles, and hands it on to their successors in its full purity, so that led by the light of the Spirit of truth, they may in proclaiming it preserve this word of God faithfully, explain it, and make it more widely known. Consequently it is not from Sacred Scripture alone that the Church draws her certainty about everything which has been revealed. Therefore both sacred tradition and Sacred Scripture are to be accepted and venerated with the same sense of loyalty and reverence.

Tradition, then, is the teaching of the apostles that preceded even the writing of the New Testament books. For decades before Christians possessed any written gospels, they received the fullness of the gospel of Jesus Christ. Among the *dogmata* listed by Basil as examples are the liturgical formulas and other sacramental practices, such as tracing the sign of the cross. These, he said, were passed on "in a mystery," from generation to generation.

Basil was, of course, working from a Pauline model. Though the Pauline letters do not explicitly make a distinction between scripture and tradition, they do speak of both in distinct ways, yet as dual sources of authority. In second Thessalonians we find: "stand firm and hold to the traditions which you were taught by us, either by word of mouth or by letter" (2 Thess 2:15).

We find a similar dynamic at work when Paul writes, in

first Corinthians, about the passing on of the liturgy. Though Paul was not present at the Last Supper, he states that he received his teaching from the churches founded by the apostles; they, in turn, received this teaching directly from the Lord: "For I received from the Lord what I also delivered to you" (1 Cor 11:23). The Greek words Paul uses, translated as "received" and "handed on," are technical terms the rabbis of his day used to describe the keeping and teaching of sacred traditions. Paul uses these same words to describe his doctrine on Christ's death and resurrection (see 1 Cor 15:2–3). These two sacred traditions—the truth about Christ's death and resurrection and the liturgy of the eucharist—were received from the Lord and handed on by the apostles. These traditions were inseparable from and crucial to the message of salvation they preached.

In the passage from first Corinthians, Paul further speaks of the liturgical action as a proclamation: "For as often as you eat this bread and drink the cup, you proclaim the Lord's death until he comes" (1 Cor 11:26). The verb translated as "proclaim" *(katangellete)* means literally to announce the good news, and is used throughout the New Testament to mean the preaching of the gospel. Protestant commentator W. Robertson Nicoll interpreted the word, in this context, as "the active expression of *anamnesis* . . . The rite looks forward as well as backward; a rehearsal of the Passion Supper, a foretaste of the Marriage Supper of the Lamb."[4]

The rite, then, is itself a proclamation of the gospel of Jesus Christ, not only in words, but also in action; and the actions themselves are an essential part of the transmission and the content of the gospel. They are core *dogmata,* which the church passes on in a mystery. They are divinely revealed truths conveyed through time by the sacred tradition.

⁂

Pope John Paul II, in his apostolic letter on the eastern churches, *Orientale Lumen,* composed an extended meditation on the phenomenon of tradition. The church's devotion to tradition is not "nostalgia for things or forms past." It is, rather, "the living memory of the Bride, kept eternally youthful by the Love that dwells within her." Tradition, then, is *anamnesis,* a *living* memory. Tradition is, he continued,

> *a living memory of the Risen One met and witnessed to by the Apostles who passed on his living memory to their successors in an uninterrupted line, guaranteed by the apostolic succession through the laying on of hands, down to the bishops of today. . . . It is not an unchanging repetition of formulas, but a heritage which preserves its original, living kerygmatic core.*

Again and again, John Paul returned to the word "living" in his discussion of tradition and memory. He is not unique in this usage. The church, in official documents, often speaks of its "living tradition." In popular parlance, that seems an oxymoron. "Tradition," for many people, is practically defined by that which is non-living—fragments from a long-ago past, dusty scraps of parchment.

For the apostolic churches, however, tradition is something alive, something vital. The church receives its life from God the Holy Spirit, and the Spirit's movement through time is the very stuff of tradition. The Spirit gives life to tradition and makes it *living* tradition. To deny the value of tradition betrays a woeful misunderstanding of the temporal mission of the Holy Spirit.

Augustine, synthesizing the teachings of Paul, taught that the Holy Spirit is the soul of the mystical Body of Christ, which is the church. The soul is what gives life to the body.[5] When soul and body separate, death follows; the body becomes a corpse. Augustine taught, moreover, that the soul, created in the image of the Trinity, possesses three faculties: memory, intellect, and will—and the "father" of that "trinity" is memory.[6]

Again, by "memory" we should not understand the contemporary English language's reduced notion. Memory is not merely the psychological exercise of data retrieval. Memory is the faculty that tells us who we are. Without memory, I could not complete this sentence, nor could you read it. Without memory, you could not know who you are from one moment to the next. Memory, in the sense of the ancients, may be what modern psychologists and philosophers are groping toward when they speak of "identity" or "self-consciousness."

The soul of the church also possesses this faculty. Jesus

said: "But the Counselor, the Holy Spirit, whom the Father will send in my name, he will teach you all things, and bring to your *remembrance* all that I have said to you" (Jn 14:26). The church has a remembrance, and it is called the liturgy. The liturgy is the memory of the church.

It is in the liturgy that the children of God encounter the memory of their family history, and this is a work of the Spirit. "In the Liturgy of the Word the Holy Spirit 'recalls' to the assembly all that Christ has done for us. . . . the celebration 'makes a remembrance' of the marvelous works of God in an anamnesis which may be more or less developed. The Holy Spirit who thus awakens the memory of the Church then inspires thanksgiving and praise (doxology)."[7]

It is no wonder that all the apostolic churches, but especially the eastern churches, have long looked upon the epiclesis—the invocation of the Spirit—as a climactic point in the liturgy. In some eastern rites, the moment is called the *"parousia"* of the Spirit.[8]

The liturgy is the place where tradition lives, where memory lives. This was its purpose from the very beginning, when Jesus commanded his apostles to "Do this in *memory* of me." In the Old Testament, too, the one commandment that concerns the liturgy is *"Remember* the Sabbath day, and keep it holy."

Again, we must be careful not to mistake what these commands mean by remembrance. God is not urging his people to keep alive a warm nostalgia for the old days. In the liturgy, God remembers his covenant and calls the church to do the same. This does not mean that the church, or God, will forget the covenant at all other times. But in the liturgy the church commemorates, and celebrates, and preserves its identity from moment to moment.

The liturgy is, once again, where the early church kept the scriptures. Indeed, the books we know as the New Testament were canonized not so much for devotional reading—which was rare in those days before the printing press—but for liturgical proclamation. The liturgy is where most exegesis took place through much of the patristic era. The controversy over which books should be included in the Bible was, to a great extent, a running argument over which books could be read during the Mass. As Justin Martyr said in 155 A.D., one of the principal parts of the liturgy was the reading of the prophets and the "memoirs" of the apostles.

When the church reads those memories aloud, Christians share in the events, the "mysteries," of the life of Christ—again, not in a nostalgic way, but in a real and substantial way. The events are actualized for them. For the liturgy effects a re-presentation of the paschal mystery of Christ's death and resurrection, and a participation in his glory in heaven. In the Mass, Christians are caught up in the one sacrifice, which is eternal.

The liturgy is where tradition lives, where the church's memory reigns "in the Spirit." The liturgy enables Christians to remember their past, but also to remember their future. For the liturgy is pointed to eternity, where past and future converge.

What makes tradition "living" is the Spirit's indwelling

presence in the church; and it is in the divine liturgy that Christians worship "in the Spirit on the Lord's Day" (see Rev 1:10). The *Catechism* summarized this in a powerful way:

> *The Spirit and the Church cooperate to manifest Christ and his work of salvation in the liturgy. Primarily in the Eucharist, and by analogy in the other sacraments, the liturgy is the* memorial *of the mystery of salvation. The Holy Spirit is the Church's living memory.*[9]

In the liturgy, the church is most alive, because, there, the body and soul are truly one. In the liturgy, the church knows its identity and teaches more surely than in the most solemn of papal documents. Pope Pius XI said that the liturgy is the primary organ of the teaching church. "The liturgy is not the *didascalia* of this or that individual," he added, "but the *didascalia* of the church."[10]

Pius's observation is hardly a late development of doctrine. At the end of the second century, Irenaeus taught what he had learned from Polycarp, who had learned it in turn from John: "Our way of thinking is attuned to the Eucharist, and the Eucharist in turn confirms our way of thinking."[11] In the fifth century, Prosper of Aquitaine stated it more precisely: *legem credendi lex statuat supplicandi.*[12] Theology has reduced it to the shorthand principle: *lex credendi, lex orandi.* "The law of prayer is the law of faith: the Church believes as she prays. Liturgy is a constitutive element of the holy and living Tradition."[13]

History is replete with examples of this principle in action. It is foundational to John Henry Newman's argument in *An Essay on the Development of Christian Doctrine.* Newman demonstrates that many disputed doctrines—purgatory, the cult of the saints, veneration of relics, and celibacy—had been implicit in the devotions of the early Christians, long before anyone proposed them in doctrinal formulas.[14]

This "law" applied just as well to core doctrines. Christians were worshiping Jesus as divine—"singing hymns to him as to a god," said the pagan Pliny—in the earliest decades of the church. Christians proclaimed the christological prologue of John's gospel in the first generation. It would be centuries before ecumenical councils began to experiment with the language of person (*hypostasis*) and nature (*ousia*).

We know, too, that the trinitarian baptismal formula existed, evidently for centuries, before Tertullian got around to coining the term *Trinitas.* The church apparently did not await the permission of theologians before adoring the three-personed God. Yves Congar observed that the liturgy—above all other earthly institutions—*"is the principal instrument of the Church's Tradition."*[15] "The liturgy is the privileged locus of Tradition."[16]

Indeed, in some cases, liturgical expression flourished for centuries while theologians and even popes kept silent. Churches throughout the world sang hymns to the Virgin Mary as *Panagia*—All-holy—for more than a millennium before Pius IX solemnly defined the dogma of her immaculate conception.

"The law of prayer is the law of faith." It was this principle that made Robert Louis Wilken, the dean of American church historians, reconsider his separation from the Catholic tradition. When asked by a reporter to explain, Wilken

> *offered the example of a famous exchange between a Lutheran scholar and St. Robert Bellarmine in the years after the Reformation. The Lutheran, he said, argued against Eucharistic adoration on the grounds that Christ meant for the sacrament to be used, not reserved. It was, as Wilken put it, a perfectly legitimate theological point. Bellarmine's response was that the Church had adored the Eucharist for a long time, and there was no good reason to abandon the practice. In fact, Wilken argued, once the Lutherans jettisoned adoration, they developed a different Eucharistic doctrine that moved away from the enduring "real presence" of Christ. It's a case in which the tradition of the community had protected the faith.*[17]

Liturgy is the *living memory* of the church. Liturgy is where the living tradition is most alive—where life *continues,* uninterrupted and unchanged, even as it undergoes truly vital and organic development. Such development is the very proof that something is living. But tradition is only *living* tradition insofar as it is consecrated in the liturgy. This is what Christians mean when they appeal to tradition's great and golden law: *Lex orandi, lex credendi.*

The truly great repository of *lex credendi* is the lectionary. Since few people could read the scriptures and fewer still could afford to own them, most people encountered the Bible not in its canonical sequence, but in its liturgical sequence. This was true of the synagogue as well, where continuous reading of the law and the prophets was customary, with special readings for the holy days. It is certainly possible, and perhaps even likely, that a synagogue lectionary was in place in Jesus' lifetime. It is even more likely that readings were fairly fixed for the major Jewish and Christian holy days, Passover and Easter, by the end of the second century. The Babylonian Talmud (sixth century) records lectionary disputes purportedly from the early second century.[18]

Both synagogue and church tended to arrange the festal readings typologically. The ancient rabbis saw Isaac, for example, as a type of the paschal lamb, and the Passover liturgy reflected that interpretation. The Christian fathers saw both Isaac and the lamb as figures of the crucified Christ, and included both Old Testament narratives in the readings for the liturgies of Holy Week. The cycles of liturgical readings, in both synagogue and church, employed typology to convey certain ideas about the divine economy, the historical pattern of God's providential care. In the course of the liturgical year (or sometimes a two- or three-year cycle), both Jews and Christians would receive repeated exposure to the major events of salvation history. The celebration of the other rites, sacraments and sacramentals, applied the same pattern to the course of a lifetime. Because of the lectionary's unfolding, the weeks, the seasons, and the years would tell a unified, continuous story and, in the process, teach doctrine. Samson Raphael Hirsch, revered as the founder of modern Orthodox Judaism, summed it up in an aphorism: "The catechism of the Jew is the calendar."[19] That is no less true of the Christian, ancient or modern. The liturgical calendar and its lectionary remain the great watercourse for the stream of salvation history.

Pius XI spoke eloquently of the power of the liturgical calendar and the lectionary:

> For people are instructed in the truths of faith and brought to appreciate the inner joys of religion far more effectively by the annual celebration of our sacred mysteries than by any pronouncement, however weighty, of the teaching of the Church. Such pronouncements usually reach only a few and the more learned among the faithful; feasts reach them all; the former speak but once, the latter speak every year—in fact, forever.[20]

Thus the lectionary ensures the perpetual remembrance of God's covenant with humankind. Justin Martyr, mentioned earlier in this chapter, is the earliest witness to the church's use of both testaments in the Sunday liturgy. But he is soon joined by many others: Melito of Sardis, Irenaeus, Hippolytus. It is likely that Old Testament readings were standard in the church from the very beginning, even before the New Testament books were written and certainly before they were collected. Clement of Rome, writing perhaps in the late sixties A.D., draws from a thoroughgoing knowledge of the scriptures of the Jews. The Marcionite crisis, in the second century, probably made it necessary for all churches to insist upon Old Testament reading as a proof of orthodoxy. The arch-heretic Marcion taught that the Old Testament was an evil counterfeit and Yahweh a bumbling, sadistic demigod. His followers lingered around the fringes of the church for more than a century, drawing refutations from Tertullian and Irenaeus, among others. *Lex orandi* witnessed against them from the beginning. The language of doctrine followed.

Of this process, Max Thurian wrote: "Through this abundant use of the Scriptures in the liturgy, the Church in a certain manner makes a living experience of the Word of God; and this experience is the essential form of tradition. In its choice of biblical texts for the liturgy, then, the Church provides a living interpretation of the Scriptures."[21]

❧❧

Tradition, said Congar, "is an interpretation of Scripture." He then added: "tradition, however, is that interpretation of Scripture which is the interpretation of the Church." Private interpretation is eminently fallible. Biblical faith has, in every age, recognized authoritative interpreters of the covenant. Jesus said: "The scribes and the Pharisees sit on Moses' seat; so practice and observe whatever they tell you" (Mt 23:2–3). Because of their teaching office, the scribes and pharisees benefited from a certain protection of the

137

Holy Spirit, even though "they preach, but do not practice" (v. 3). The chief priest Caiaphas received a divine gift of prophecy, even as he was plotting the murder of Jesus, simply because of the sacred office he held, however unworthily: "He did not say this of his own accord, but being high priest that year he prophesied that Jesus should die for the nation" (Jn 11:51). Again, the authority of these men did not depend so much upon their virtues, their learning, or their wisdom as upon their office.

The structure of covenantal authority did not pass away with the coming of Jesus Christ. At the last supper, Jesus told his apostles: "I assign [diatithemai] to you, as my Father assigned [dietheto] to me, a kingdom, that you may eat and drink at my table in my kingdom, and sit on thrones judging the twelve tribes of Israel" (Lk 22:29–30). The Greek can be literally translated as "I covenant to you, as my Father covenanted to me, a kingdom."

In the Acts of the Apostles, we see priestly authority passed to the apostolic college. The opening chapter discusses it as episkopen, the public office of an overseer (v. 20). In succeeding chapters, the apostles, in turn, bestow authority and power upon elders (presbuteroi) and deacons (diakonoi). Consider the story of the Ethiopian eunuch (Acts 8:26ff). The eunuch is reading aloud a scroll of the prophet Isaiah. He is a believer, who can read; he has the means to own copies of the scriptures, and he has the leisure to study them. Still, Philip asks him: "Do you understand what you are reading?" And the eunuch replies: "How can I, unless someone guides me?" Philip begins from Isaiah and tells him "the good news of Jesus." Where private interpretation had failed, the apostle's authority taught infallibly, led and preserved from error by the Holy Spirit. Correct interpretation required the mediation of the church. The story concludes, appropriately enough, with a sacramental liturgy—the baptism of the eunuch.

The apostles possessed the spiritual gifts to sanctify, to teach, and to rule. Thus they had the authority to proclaim the gospel and preside over the liturgy. They communicated this authority liturgically, by the laying on of hands (Acts 14:23; 2 Cor 8:19; 2 Tim 1:6). They exercised their teaching authority individually and by meeting at council, presided over by Peter (Acts 15:6ff).

Thus the early fathers took care to show their succession from the apostles. Clement traced his Roman pedigree back to Peter and Paul; Irenaeus traced his own lineage, through Polycarp, to John.[22] Irenaeus is, in R. M. Grant's phrase, the "father of authoritative exegesis,"[23] the champion of the clergy's right and duty to proclaim and interpret the scriptures "in the church."

> *Therefore, one must listen carefully to the presbyters in the church, the ones who have received their succession from the apostles, as we have shown, and who have obtained, together with the succession of the episcopacy, the sure charism of truth according to the good pleasure of the Father. Others, however, who draw back from the original succession and as-*

*semble wherever they please, must be looked upon with sus-
picion; they should be regarded as heretics pursuing perverse
ideas, or as schismatics, puffed up and self-pleasing.*[24]

The clergy who could preside over the liturgical assembly, the clergy who could proclaim and interpret the scriptures with authority, were those who had succession from
the apostles—that is, the bishops. The bishops alone held the
right, by virtue of their office, to teach doctrine, to preside
over the liturgy, to proclaim and interpret the scriptures, and
to discipline the faithful. They could delegate many of those
duties to the priests, and some to the deacons. Ignatius of
Antioch said, in 107 A.D.: "Let that be deemed a valid eucharist which is under the bishop, or one to whom he has
entrusted it."[25]

We have touched upon the interrelationship of the three
sources of authority in the church: scripture, tradition, and
magisterium. In the Acts of the Apostles, as through the
patristic era, we can see how much all three depend upon
a developed pneumatology. The Spirit who inspired the
scriptures and animates tradition is the same Spirit who preserves the apostolic teaching authority—the church's magisterium.

In the nineteenth century, at the beginning of the great
modern patristic and liturgical retrievals, Dom Prosper
Gueranger wrote: "It is in the liturgy that the Spirit who inspired the Scriptures speaks again: the liturgy is Tradition itself at its highest degree of power and solemnity." Yves
Congar read Gueranger's definition and pronounced that

"No finer expression of the truth could be found."[26] I have to agree.

Scripture is not self-interpreting; its meaning is not self-evident. Like all literary and legislative texts, it requires an interpretive community, and that is the church. The further people have strayed from the church, the bishops, and the liturgical assembly, the less reliable were their scriptural interpretations, the more heterodox their teaching. This, too, is *Lex orandi, lex credendi* at work. Cardinal Ratzinger wrote:

> *In the Catholic Church the principle of "tradition" refers, not only and not even in the first place, to the permanency of ancient doctrines or texts which have been handed down, but to a certain way of co-ordinating the living word of the Church and the decisive written word of scripture. . . . The Bible is lived and interpreted in a way that binds. This interpretation forms a historical continuity, setting fixed standards but never itself reaching a final point at which it belongs only to the past. "Revelation" is closed but interpretation which binds is not.[27]*

I cannot help invoking, once again, the story with which I began this book, Athanasius' account of Anthony's hearing of the gospel. On that passage, Bertrand de Margerie commented: "the biblical culture which Athanasius extols . . . is not independent of the Church; rather, it is above all an ecclesial and liturgical reading that is fostered. He is urging those living the solitary life to read the Bible with the Church."[28]

Scripture must be read "with the church." The Methodist theologian Stanley Hauerwas called Martin Luther's doctrine of *sola scriptura* "a heresy rather than a help," precisely because "It assumes that the text of Scripture makes sense separate from a Church that gives it sense."[29] He noted also that this presupposition is shared as well by biblical fundamentalists and biblical critics; both "make the Church incidental."[30]

It has been said that "the history of doctrine is the history of exegesis."[31] But, through the first millennium of Christianity, we cannot find any widespread and sustained efforts in scientific exegesis. To read scripture "with the church" was to read it or hear it in the liturgy. Apostolic and patristic exegesis took place not primarily in the classroom or in the monastic cell, but in the public reading and proclamation of scripture in the liturgy. "The Fathers are pastors," wrote Congar. "Their treatises are sermons."[32]

Even today, "with the church" remains functionally equivalent to "in the liturgy." The liturgy is, as Pius XI taught us, the primary organ of the magisterium. The liturgy is, in the words of Congar, the principal instrument and the privileged locus of tradition. The liturgy is, as we saw in the scriptural apocalypses of Stephen and John, the place where we still encounter God's word "in the Spirit."

CHAPTER 9

APOCALYPSE AND MYSTAGOGY

L ITURGY IS THE place where the scriptures emerge into light. Liturgy is the place where tradition lives and where the church teaches most surely. Liturgy is the place where the stream of salvation history runs swift and clear—sweeping Christians into the current of the divine and sacramental economy. Divine liturgy is the place where Christians, many millennia after the fall, the flood, the exodus, and the passion can participate directly in the fulfillment of the biblical types. Liturgy is the place where God's people have always gone to hear the covenant and to renew the covenant, with all their heart and mind, soul and body.

Yet, with the ascension of Jesus Christ into heaven, liturgy came to stand for something more than it had ever meant in sacred history. For, in heaven, according to the earliest Christian beliefs, Jesus stands forever as priest and as victim. The Christian people, sharing his nature by baptism, share in his priesthood and offer their own lives with his as an oblation. Jesus Christ presides over a liturgy that unites heaven and earth. Listen to Martimort:

By his victorious ascension Christ had broken through the boundaries of creation; he had triumphed over time and taken human nature with him into the heavenly sanctuary where Israel had accustomed itself to seeing myriads of angels performing their service around Adonai. Henceforth, those on earth would not simply imitate what was done perfectly on 'the mountain of God,' in heavenly Zion; they would actually take part in that solemn liturgy.[1]

These are the themes presented in most powerful terms in the biblical books of Hebrews and Revelation, but especially Revelation. Martimort wrote: "What the pattern of the tabernacle shown on the mountain (Ex 25:9) was for Moses, the Letter to the Hebrews and the Apocalypse are for the Church."[2] Little wonder, then, that "The spirit of the Letter to the Hebrews and the Apocalypse enlivens the early Eucharistic Prayers of all the Christian rites and permeates their ceremonial."[3] Both books describe, in figurative and theological language, what is continuous in the covenants, old and new, and in the liturgies, old and new—and what is discontinuous. Both books address the question: In what sense did the new fulfill the old?

In the early centuries, the mainstream of Christianity rejected two proposed answers to that question. One would come to be known as the "Ebionite" solution—a Jewish-Christian model that saw Christ's fulfillment as predominantly restorative of the old covenant and its law. The other proposal would eventually coalesce into Marcionism—an anti-Jewish model that saw Christ's fulfillment as transformative—an utter rejection and replacement of Israel, the God of Israel, his liturgy, his law, and his scripture. Though the names "Ebionite" and "Marcionite" were not applied until the second century, the seeds of these movements were certainly present in the first generations. The problem of fulfillment is at the heart of Paul's arguments in Romans and Galatians; and it is the very stuff of the recurrent disputes in the Acts of the Apostles.

The matter is settled definitively, if mysteriously, in Hebrews and Revelation. There, the church articulates an understanding of fulfillment that it is both transformative and restorative—a transfiguration of the law, the liturgy, and the kingdom of Israel.

The body of Christ can serve as a paradigm. When the gospels portrayed Jesus in his post-resurrection appearances, he possessed the same body that had been beaten and bled only days before; it was restored, and yet it was also transformed. In a similar way, as the earthly temple would be destroyed, so by Christ's resurrection and ascension it would be both restored and transformed in heaven. At his ascension, Christ represented the church as he entered within the veil, once for all; and so he elevated the covenant worship of the assembly. As priest in heaven, he possessed the same body as when he had celebrated the old Passover on earth, but it was now transformed and transfigured. In Revelation, he appeared offering himself to the Father as a perpetual oblation, "a lamb standing, as if slain" (Rev 5:6)—his body is restored and yet transformed.

Jesus Christ is both victim and priest in the heavenly liturgy, which by his ascension he united with the earthly liturgy. Thus, it was in and through his body that he transformed the old covenant into the new, the old liturgy into the new, the old law into the new. The eucharistic body of Christ, then, is not simply a reappearance of Jesus' earthly body. This *parousia* is restorative, and it is transformative.

It is the presence of Christ—as "a high priest forever" (Heb 6:20) and a sacrifice "without blemish" (Heb 9:14)—that makes the difference. And this is what both Hebrews and Revelation communicate in their visions of the heavenly liturgy. Both books provide Christianity's first and foundational mystagogy—a divinely revealed "guidance in the mysteries." Both present a vision of the sacramental economy as it came to fulfillment in heaven and earth.

Now, we may anticipate the most obvious objection. Some may scoff at this suggestion, with Martin Luther, who went so far as to question the canonical status of John's Apocalypse. Luther complained that "A Revelation should reveal something."[4] Revelation is indeed a difficult and sometimes obscure book.

The purpose of mystagogy, however, is not to dispel the divine mystery. Still less should a mystagogical work rationalize mystery away—or function as an extended exercise in cryptography. True mystagogy respects the divine mystery, even as it guides Christians into a more profound experience of, and participation in, that very mystery. The *Catechism* (n. 2777) captures this sense beautifully:

From the burning bush Moses heard a voice saying to him, "Do not come near; put off your shoes from your feet, for the place on which you are standing is holy ground" (Ex 3:5). Only Jesus could cross that threshold of the divine holiness, for "when he had made purification for sins," he brought us into the Father's presence: "Here am I, and the children God has given me" (Heb 1:3; 2:13).

That is the purpose of the great mystagogical teachings of the biblical and patristic ages, from Hebrews and Revelation through Cyril and Ambrose to Maximus Confessor and Nicholas Cabisalas. One and all, they reveal the mystery, without reducing it. In revealing the mystery, they reveal the new place of mankind in the covenantal and sacramental economy. Baptized into Christ's death, Christians are made "sons in the Son"—children of God. They enter the mystery, liturgically and sacramentally, with Christ himself.

In the mystagogy of the fathers, there are usually two well-developed components: an explanation of the sacramental rites, and an unveiling of the mysteries. Mystagogy of the sacraments leads believers to a deeper understanding of the liturgy and its scriptural and historical roots. The revelation of the mysteries, mystagogy proper, leads to a deeper understanding of the mysteries invisible to the eye, but perceptible by faith—e.g., the eucharistic *parousia* of Jesus Christ, the heavenly liturgy, the presence of the angels and saints, and the fatherly Providence of God.

True mystagogy, then, unveils not only the rite, but the reality it represents (and re-presents). Mystagogy unveils not only a present ceremony, but an unfolding economy that encompasses past and future history. The subject of mystagogy is not only the sacraments, but primarily the mysteries.

But it often begins with the rites, though these require a simultaneous beginning in scripture. As Congar wrote in his monumental *Tradition and Traditions*: "It is evident to anyone who is acquainted with Scripture and the liturgy that the latter is woven out of scriptural texts and allusions. . . . Many liturgical gestures simply reproduce those mentioned in the Bible. Further, the liturgy's *ethos* is in continuity with that of Scripture."[5]

It is perhaps belaboring the obvious to point out that most of the liturgy is composed of scriptural texts. Consider a sampling from the Latin rite:

Trinitarian blessing	Mt 28:19
Sign of the cross	Rev 7:3; 9:4; 14:1; typified in Ezek 9:4
Amen	1 Chr 16:36b
Apostolic greeting	2 Cor 13:14
Dominus vobiscum	Lk 1:28; 2 Thess 3:16; 2 Tim 4:22; Ruth 2:4
Confiteor	After Ps 51; Jas 5:16; et al.
Kyrie	Mt 17:15; Mt 20:31; Ps 123:3

Gloria	Lk 2:14; many texts in Revelation
First reading	Usually from OT, Acts, epistles, or Revelation
Responsorial psalm	A psalm or biblical canticle
Second reading	Usually from NT books (not the gospels)
Alleluia	Rev 19:1–6; Tob 13:18
Gospel	From the gospels
Sursum corda	Lam 3:41
Sanctus	Rev 4:8; Is 6:3; Mk 11:9–10; Ps 118:26
Eucharistic prayer	The heart is 1 Cor 11:23–26; many other passages
The great amen	Rev 5:14
The Lord's Prayer	Mt 6:9–13
Sign of Peace	Jn 14:27; 20:19
Agnus Dei	Jn 1:29; Rev 5:6 and elsewhere
Ecce Agnus Dei	Rev 19:9
Domine, non sum dignus	Mt 8:8
Dismissal	Lk 7:50; 2 Chr 35:3
Deo gratias	2 Cor 9:15

To subject any of the eucharistic prayers to the same analysis would be to double the size of the chart. Needless to say, the Byzantine, Malabar, Maronite, Melkite, and other rites employ the same density of biblical quotation and allusion.

A mystagogy of the rites should begin from these scriptural beginnings, not for the sake of proof-texting, but for the sake of historical grounding. Again, the liturgy is the *Sitz im Leben* of the Bible and of the fathers. It is the principle and the place of continuity for Christian tradition and interpretation.

The chart above shows how intimately the biblical Book of Revelation interrelates with the earthly liturgy. We could drawn up a similar chart tracking the liturgical elements in the Apocalypse (and indeed it has been done).[6] It is difficult to say which way the current of influence runs stronger, from the earthly rites to the Seer's vision, or vice versa. One thing is certain: the canon's final coda makes little sense apart from the liturgical worship of God's covenant people. Leonard Thompson wrote that "Even a cursory reading of the Book of Revelation shows the presence of liturgical language set in worship."

> In both Revelation and the early church, worship serves as the setting in which eschatological narratives (such as the Book of Revelation itself) unfold. Furthermore, in both Revelation and the churches of Asia Minor, worship realizes the kingship of God and his just judgement; through liturgical celebration eschatological expectations are experienced presently. Hymns, thanksgivings, doxologies, and acclamations realize in the context of worship the eschatological message. . . . The Book of Revelation, by functioning in communal worship of Asia Minor as heavenly worship functions in the book itself, links heaven and earth. The work mediates its own message."[7]

The liturgy illuminates both the literal-historical sense and the theological and mystical senses of the Book of Revelation. Even commentators apart from the liturgical traditions have, with laborious effort, reconstructed this fact. Oddly enough, commentators within the liturgical traditions have grown somewhat fearful of the Apocalypse. Ian Boxall, in his remarkable study, *Revelation: Vision and Insight,* noted that "The Orthodox Church forbids the reading of the book during public worship, reserving the book for the spiritually mature." While acknowledging the dangers inherent in popular misunderstanding of Revelation's sometimes violent text, Boxall says, nevertheless, that liturgical suppression merely exacerbates the problem. "To remove such texts from liturgical use . . . will not necessarily mean that people will no longer read them, but that they will be read in a dangerously uninformed and unreflective manner. A liturgical context for reading, however, can minimize these dangers."[8]

What actualizes the Book of Revelation is the earthly liturgy, because the church's earthly liturgy actualizes the heavenly liturgy on earth. To participate in the church's worship is to share the prostrations and praises of the angels and saints. To read the Apocalypse liturgically is to begin to understand the Apocalypse, and how the rites of heaven direct the course of earthly history. The household of God observes an *oikonomia*—literally, a "household law." It is evident in the typological pattern of salvation history, which continues now in the church's liturgy.

The eschatological orientation—and eschatological immanence—of the liturgy is as evident in the most primitive liturgies as it is in the New Testament's apocalypses. It is evident as well in the church's most recent teaching. The unity of heavenly and earthly liturgy is a theme that has dominated the documents of the Catholic Church since the Second Vatican Council. Nowhere is this as evident as in the *Catechism of the Catholic Church*. Consider just a sampling of the *Catechism*'s doctrine (all emphases are in the original):

> *"In the earthly liturgy we share in a foretaste of that heavenly liturgy which is celebrated in the Holy City of Jerusalem toward which we journey as pilgrims, where Christ is sitting at the right hand of God, Minister of the sanctuary and of the true tabernacle."* (CCC, n. 1090; *quoting* Sacrosanctum Concilium 8)

> *"[T]hrough her liturgical actions the pilgrim Church already participates, as by a foretaste, in the heavenly liturgy."* (CCC, n. 1111)

> *"Liturgy is an 'action' of the* whole Christ (Christus totus). *Those who even now celebrate it without signs are already in the heavenly liturgy, where celebration is wholly communion and feast."* (CCC n. 1136)

> *"The liturgy is the work of the whole Christ, head and body. Our high priest celebrates it unceasingly in the heavenly liturgy, with the holy Mother of God, the apostles, all the saints, and the multitude of those who have already entered the kingdom."* (CCC, n. 1187)

*"Finally, by the Eucharistic celebration we already unite
ourselves with the heavenly liturgy and anticipate eternal
life, when God will be all in all." (CCC, n. 1326)*[9]

To the modern western mind—acclimated, as it is, to
non-liturgical varieties of Christianity—this vision of worship can seem startling, and perhaps dubious. It has been the
constant norm, however, in the apostolic eastern churches.
In the Byzantine and West Syrian traditions, the pervasive
belief in the actualization of the heavenly liturgy has had a
profound effect on all the liturgical arts, from hymnody to
church architecture and decoration.[10] Pope John Paul II, in
his apostolic letter *Orientale Lumen,* wrote of the Byzantine
liturgy: "The lengthy duration of the celebrations, the repeated invocations, everything expresses gradual identifica-
tion with the mystery celebrated with one's whole person.
Thus the prayer of the Church already becomes participation in the heavenly liturgy, an anticipation of the final beat-
itude." A. G. Martimort observed that "The Roman rite is
more restrained but no less realistic about the supraterrestrial
character of the liturgy."[11]

What the Apocalypse shows is the definitive consummation
of the covenant. Thus the number seven dominates the
book: seven churches, the seven spirits and seven torches of
fire before the throne, the seven lampstands, the seven spirits of the son of man and the seven stars in his right hand,

the seven seals, seven angels that stand before God, the seven horns and seven eyes of the Lamb, the seven thunders, seven trumpets, and seven chalices of God's wrath. The overwhelming message is that the son of man has definitively renewed the covenant. He has sevened himself by the liturgical offering of his body, once for all.

Revelation shows that the historic covenants found recapitulation in Christ. Like Adam, Jesus received the "tree of life" (Rev 22:2), thus renewing God's original covenant with the human family. As the unblemished passover lamb (Rev 5:6), Jesus fulfilled the Mosaic covenant before going on to inherit a promised land for Israel; as he and his saints occupy heaven, the blast of seven trumpets (a liturgical act), brings down the walls of the earthly city (Rev 8–9; cf. Jos 6:3–7). Like David his ancestor, Jesus ascended the throne "to rule all the nations with a rod of iron" (Rev 12:5).

In Revelation, we see the perfect fulfillment of God's covenant with his people. Every previous fulfillment, in the Old Testament, had been real, but also partial, and thus incomplete. So each covenant fulfillment was a type, driven forward, by way of anticipation, toward something greater—yet still only partial, still incomplete, still pointing to the future. Ultimately, the *parousia* stands as the final cause, the cause of all previous causes. It is the eucharistic *parousia,* in which Christ comes and breaks open the scriptures (Rev 6). But even the eucharistic *parousia* points forward to a plenary *parousia*—a day when Christ will come in glory, and we will see him as he is. G. K. Beale speaks of this final *parousia* in profound and moving terms:

> *When Christ appears, he will not descend from the sky over Boston or London or New York City or Hong Kong or any other localized area. When he appears, the present dimension will be ripped away, and Christ will be manifest to all eyes throughout the earth (see Mt 24:27). . . . If John were living today, he might use the analogy of a stage curtain with pictures on it, which is drawn from both sides to reveal the actors behind it. In short, the present physical reality will in some way disappear and the formerly hidden heavenly dimension, where Christ and God dwell, will be revealed.*[12]

Mystagogy is what keeps the church in typological balance. The present state remains penultimate. Christians now receive God's heavenly life in the eucharist, but through transitory earthly forms that are, nevertheless, fully able to communicate divine sonship.

This is the dynamism that drives history—the eschatological teleology of the covenant sequence. The economy itself is the key. It is an unfolding process of gradual and cumulative development. Each stage is anticipated in prior stages, but each stage points forward to something greater.

Mystagogy, based on the biblical Apocalypse, keeps that eschatological tension here and now. The end was the cause from the beginning. Says the *Catechism*: "From the beginning until the end of time the whole of God's work is a *blessing*. From the liturgical poem of the first creation to the canticles of the heavenly Jerusalem, the inspired authors proclaim the plan of salvation as one vast divine blessing" (CCC n. 1079).

The human person, most especially, was created for the

sake of worship. The priest says as much in a preface of the eucharistic prayer: "You made man the steward of creation, to praise you . . . with all the angels in their song of joy: Holy, Holy, Holy."[13] And in its liturgical consummation all the world is manifest in its created and perfected form: "creation is revealed for what it is: a complex whole which finds its perfection, its purpose in the liturgy alone. This is why *the liturgy is heaven on earth* [emphasis mine]."[14]

"For the creation waits with eager longing," said St. Paul, "for the *apocalypse*—the revealing—of the sons of God" (Rom 8:19).

The liturgy reveals the children of God. The liturgy reveals the kingdom of God. The liturgy reveals the word of God most perfectly because, in the liturgy, the Word of God himself is present as the hermeneutical key.

This is the stuff of economy, typology, mystagogy. In the fourth century, the Bordeaux pilgrim traveled to Jerusalem where she witnessed the mystagogical preaching of the city's bishop. (Was it Cyril himself?) She described the scene in warm detail:

> *And while the bishop discusses and sets forth each point, the voices of those who applaud are so loud that they can be heard outside the church. And truly the mysteries are so unfolded that there is no one unmoved at the things that he hears to be so explained.*[15]

Heaven has come to earth, and hearts rise up to heaven. Is it any wonder they applauded?

CHAPTER 10

ETCHED IN MEMORY

THE METROPOLITAN MUSEUM'S collection of early Christian art stands as a testimony of the ancient Church's life and biblical interpretation. It is no small collection—arrayed in two corridors and the room between them—and it serves as a time capsule, really. Many of the materials were unearthed only recently, in the "treasure" stashes of the churches of the eastern Mediterranean, the hoards that were buried by bishops and priests during the Islamic invasions of the seventh century. When the priests died, sometimes as martyrs, their secrets died with them, only to be revealed more than a millennium later.

As the Arab armies approached, the clergy gathered together all that was of value to their community—the towns and cities of the lands that are now Syria, Turkey, Egypt, and Iraq. Today any casual visitor can see those items arrayed in splendor. They are, overwhelmingly, liturgical items: chalices, ciboria, censers, pyxes, processional crosses, holy water flasks, icons, and the elaborately embossed covers of gospel books. Most are richly decorated with scenes from the Old and New Testaments.

For the purposes of this study, one vessel in particular stands out. It is a pyx carved from ivory circa 500 A.D. Four inches high and lidded, it was likely used either to reserve the eucharist or to carry the sacrament to Christians who were sick and homebound.

What is most remarkable, however, is the decoration of the pyx, which stands as a monument to the ancient church's mystagogy. One side of the vessel recalls us to Luke 24, the chapter we examined early in this book: here we see two of the female disciples standing at the empty tomb of Jesus Christ. A turn of the artifact shows us another scene, depicted so similarly as to invite the drawing of an analogy. Once again we see the same two women, only now they stand with swinging censers, flanking the sanctuary of a church. A baldacchino frames the altar on which a gospel book sits enthroned. A hanging lamp illumines the book below.

This biblical and liturgical treasure brings us back once again not only to the post-resurrection chapter of Luke, but to the three themes we discussed in that context: economy, typology, and mystagogy. For the pyx portrays a key element of classic Antiochene mystagogy: the typological connection between the tomb of Christ and the church's altar of sacrifice, between the resurrected body of Christ and the eucharistic body of Christ.[1] Within the sanctuary, the mysteries of salvation history are illuminated and extended through the sacramental liturgy and the proclamation of the scriptures. History and eternity meet. The believer dies, rises, and ascends with Christ, and so heaven and earth unite in liturgical praise. The great (though controversial) Antiochene, Theodore of Mopsuestia, preached it well in his mystagogical homilies: "Every time the liturgy of this awesome sacrifice is performed . . . we must think of ourselves in our imagination as people present in heaven; by faith we sketch in our minds a vision of heavenly realities."[2]

Through the liturgy, Christians are simultaneously present in heaven and present in the mainstream of salvation history. Resurrection is both a historical type and an antitype that is both sacramental and eschatological. This is the very meaning of the sacramental economy.

❧

What is beautifully preserved in that ancient ivory is what historical and literary study of scripture has, for the past century, been laboriously reconstructing—though the liturgical traditions have never really lost their grasp of it.

Principles of the "scientific" study of scripture, or "critical exegesis," are concerned (1) with the form and composition of a given work—how the texts were composed and handed down to us; and (2) with the meaning of a canonical work in the context of its original composition—the intentions of the author, the reception by its original audience, and the cultural milieu at the time of composition and transmission.

When scholars approach scripture according to these methods, and without strong biases—even without any sense that these are divinely inspired texts—they tend to see certain patterns emerge. Form-critical study, for example, has led us to discern a liturgical form of scripture and the liturgical purpose of the canon. Critical exegesis has helped us to see that—along with the liturgical form, function, and purpose of scripture—there is a liturgical "trajectory" to the narrative content of scripture.

What we see, then, drawing on the best insights of historical and literary study, suggests the outlines of a new, emerging method—a hermeneutic that we could describe as *liturgical* or *mystagogic*. This mystagogic hermeneutic makes us sensitive to certain aspects of the text—again, aspects suggested when the texts are read, not necessarily with the faith of the church, but simply as the texts present themselves and are understood by the best critical methods.

We can approach our study of scripture, then, as a threefold movement: from (1) literary sense to (2) historical truth to (3) divine meaning. The literary sense of scripture gives us an historical truth, and that truth presents itself to us as the divine meaning of scripture.

These three movements correspond well to our three themes of economy, typology, and mystagogy. For the literal sense of the entire biblical canon is the divine economy; the historical truth of the economy follows a typological pattern of promise and fulfillment; and, finally, the divine meaning, which was hidden for ages in mystery, is what Christ reveals mystagogically and sacramentally in the New Covenant.

We find this concept crystallized and codified in *Dei Verbum,* the Second Vatican Council's Dogmatic Constitution on Divine Revelation. Article 12 begins with a qualified endorsement of critical methods: "since God speaks in sacred scripture through men in human fashion, the interpreter of Sacred Scripture, in order to see clearly what God wanted to communicate to us, should carefully investigate what meaning the sacred writers really intended." The constitution specifies various types of analysis of literary form and style.

Article 12 culminates, however, in the establishment of three theological criteria for interpreting scripture. The *Catechism of the Catholic Church* extracts those criteria and distills them into imperative statements:

1. "Be especially attentive 'to the content and unity of the whole Scripture' " (CCC, n. 112).
2. "Read the Scripture within 'the living Tradition of the whole Church' " (CCC, n. 113). This tradition finds its supreme expression in the church's liturgy.
3. "Be attentive to the analogy of faith"—that is, the "coherence of the truths of faith among themselves and within the whole of revelation" (CCC, n. 114).

Once again, we can see the correspondence of this "triad" with the two triads mentioned earlier. The Bible's "content and unity" refers specifically to the *literary sense* of scripture, the *divine economy,* the "plot" that unifies all the individual books as well as the two testaments. Reading scripture within the mainstream of *tradition* means reading it as salvation *history*—and thus reading it *typologically,* as it appears in the liturgy and in the lectionary. Finally, the "analogy of faith" concerns itself precisely with the inner coherence of the Bible's *divine meaning,* which we discover through *mystagogy.*

Applying these principles, interpretive tradition avoids the hazards of both literalism and allegorism. At the same time, it prevents the excesses of corrosive criticism, the infinite regress of systematic doubt.

Tradition insists upon the foundational necessity of the literal-historical sense of the text of scripture. Hugh of St. Victor gave this principle its most lapidary expression: *historia fundamentum est.*[3] At the very start of his *Summa Theologica*, Thomas Aquinas provided the logical corollary: "all the senses are founded on one—the literal—from which alone can any argument be drawn, and not from those intended in allegory."[4]

Far from deprecating Israel's history, Christian interpretation should seek to preserve and even exalt the historical and literary integrity of the Old Testament. Otherwise, Christian liturgy—which depends upon deeply historical concepts such as *anamnesis* and covenant—makes no sense at all. The church's life, in all its sacramental richness, depends upon a full and vibrant appreciation of the odyssey of the people of God through history. The liturgy represents the persistence of the corporate memory of God's people, and this memory—profoundly scriptural, profoundly ritual—is essential to Christian identity. For the church is incarnational, as deeply human as it is ineradicably divine, and man does not live by bread alone. Humanity lives by memory every bit as much as it lives by bread. Deprived of memory, anything human sinks first into disorder, then dementia, and finally oblivion. Classic Christianity celebrates the fullness of the historical sense of scripture, even as it professes Christ's transcendence of history.

Thus, Christian interpretive tradition affirms the history of Israel on that history's own terms. Israel's redemption from

Egypt, for example, was a true redemption; Israel's worship in the Jerusalem temple was true worship. Nevertheless, the Christ-event has enabled the church to discern previously unknowable significance (and significations) in the events of Old Testament history. The end of the story is the hermeneutical key to all previous events, from the beginning.

The emphasis on the literal sense does not, however, rule out other "senses" of scripture; nor does it preclude any "spiritual exegesis" of biblical texts. Indeed, there are times when the literal truth of a New Testament text is itself a moral or allegorical exegesis of the Old Testament. Thus, following the New Testament model, Christian interpreters have traditionally discerned two "senses" of scripture, the literal and the spiritual. The spiritual sense has often been further divided into three: the *allegorical,* which finds a christological meaning in Old Testament texts; the *moral* (or *tropological),* which brings out examples of just action; and the *anagogical,* which reveals the significance in light of eternity and eschatology. Again, these are not invented categories; the New Testament itself is the great exemplar of simultaneous literal and spiritual exegesis. Allegorical readings, for example, are plentiful in Paul's epistles and even identified as such in Galatians 4:24. In 1 Corinthians 5–11, Paul offers a tropological reading of the Old Testament, rooted in the sacraments. The Apocalypse is, from end to end, an anagogical reading of salvation history. The *Catechism* (nn. 115–118) has sketched out scripture's literal and spiritual senses, concluding with a fairly clear mandate taken verbatim from *Dei Verbum:*

It is the task of exegetes to work, according to these rules, toward a better understanding and explanation of Sacred Scripture in order that their research may help the Church to form a firmer judgment. For, of course, all that has been said about the manner of interpreting Scripture is ultimately subject to the judgment of the Church which exercises the divinely conferred commission and ministry of watching over and interpreting the Word of God.[5]

Scientific and literary study of scripture need not lead interpreters away from tradition. Indeed, its techniques—when applied by the most rigorous and honest practitioners—confirm the details that tradition has kept for millennia in the heart of the church. Scientific exegesis has taken Christian interpreters around the world in order to arrive, again, at their own home, and to see it for the first time.

❧❧

These movements represent true progress not only for the academy, but for the church as well—specifically as the communion of saints.

Scripture is ordered to communion. This is evident in the content of the Christian canon, which culminates in the Marriage Supper of the Lamb. It is equally evident in the traditional structure of Christian liturgy, which runs from the liturgy of the word to the liturgy of the eucharist. There is a certain covenantal logic to the sequence. Consider an analogous covenant: the marriage bond is ratified by words and then consummated in bodily communion. In a similar way, the new covenant of Jesus Christ is ratified by the dialogue of reading and response, and then consummated in eucharistic communion. There is something inexorable about this sequence, and it affects even our extra-liturgical reading of scripture. As Lucien Deiss has noted:

> *This constant reference to the covenant clearly does not imply that every celebration of the word must end with the sacramental Eucharist. But it does tend, at least virtually, toward the Eucharist. Let us say that it is oriented toward the grace of the Eucharist or, if you prefer, to a 'spiritual communion' when sacramental communion is not to be available.*[6]

Scripture leads its reader, or hearer, to a theophany—and, more than a theophany, a participation in the divine nature (see 2 Peter 1:4), a communion with the holy. For, according to biblical religion, God alone is holy (1 Samuel 2:2; Rev 14:4), but he deigns to share his nature with his chosen people. Through this communion they become his holy people.

Holiness is something commonly misconceived in the popular mind and even in serious scholarship. These misconceptions tend to fall into two categories: the ethical and the experiential (or phenomenological). The first confuses holiness with righteousness, moral rectitude. The second reduces it to a subjective sense of awe in the presence of the numinous and a corresponding sense of one's own smallness before the Almighty. Righteousness and humility can be preconditions for theophany, and they can be immediate or eventual effects of theophany. But they are not identical with God's self-revelation or life-giving presence.

The gift of self is at the heart of the covenant. For a covenant greatly exceeds a contract. A contract is an exchange of goods and services ("This is yours, and that is mine"), but a covenant is an exchange of persons ("I am yours, and you are mine"). The new relationship is a family bond: "you shall be my people, and I will be your God" (Ezek 36:28). Those who enter the covenant dwell in the house of the Lord and live in his family.

To live in God's family means to be set apart, to be purified. This has been a defining characteristic of biblical religion, from the ritual ablutions of the Old Testament to the baptism of the New. There is a common "sacramental" theology implicit in the biblical record—even in the Old Testament, even in Leviticus. Jacob Milgrom wrote: "Theology is what Leviticus is all about. It pervades every chapter and almost every verse. It is not expressed in pronouncements (i.e., words) but embedded in ritual."[7] It is ritual that brings about purity, ritual that transfers holiness from God to humankind.

The place set apart for liturgy, the place of theophany, the "house of the Lord," is the temple. Again, only those who share God's holiness may approach. Here is Milgrom again: "the *sancta* of the Bible can cause death to the unwary and the impure who approach them without regard for the regulations that govern their usage."[8] The scriptures are replete with examples of this, from the unholy fire of Nadab and Abihu (Lev 10:1–3, 8–10) to the impurity and idolatry of

Belshazzar, who finds himself accursed for profaning the vessels of the Jerusalem temple (Dan 5:22–23).

The liturgical proclamation of scripture provides a necessary purification and preparation for the temple's theophany. The liturgy of the word—the "mass of the catechumens"—keeps worshipers from entering unwary or impure into the *divine liturgy* that is the anaphora. Christian liturgy is the place of the "re-templing" that came with the new covenant. The continuity is evident to Jewish scholars, such as Baruch Levine, who observed the clear connection between Israel's sacrificial liturgy and the sacrifice and communion of Mass.[9]

The reading of scripture is oriented to this communion, which is, again, a "holy" communion, a partaking of the divine nature. But it is still more than that: It is what tradition means by the *communio sanctorum*—not merely the communion of saints, but the communion of *sancta,* of all that is made holy by the presence of God. Jerome wrote to Pope Damasus of the need "to instruct by the authority of scripture ignorant people in all the churches concerning the reverence with which they must handle holy things and minister at Christ's altar; and to impress upon them that the sacred chalices, veils and other accessories used in the celebration of the Lord's passion are not mere lifeless and senseless objects devoid of holiness, but that rather, from their association with the body and blood of the Lord, they are to be venerated with the same awe as the body and the blood themselves."[10] The "saints" themselves, of course, were to be treated with even greater care, and not simply those in heaven, but the saints on earth as well, no matter their station in life. The *Di-*

dascalia Apostolorum commanded: "Widows and orphans are to be revered as the altar of sacrifice."[11]

Holiness then leads to certain ethical behavior, to a certain social engagement, but again it is not identical with "good morals" or "social justice." It cannot be achieved by mere human effort, but only by the divinely revealed, sacramental means.

The biblical witness to holiness is theophany, epiphany, presence. The burning bush and Mount Sinai are set apart from other places on the planet because of God's *parousia,* his presence, his coming, his glory. It is God's glory that shone in Moses' face and made him holy, like God.

God's holy ones, his saints, are not just good citizens and upright people. They are set apart for coming into the divine presence and mediating that presence. Sainthood includes ethical and experiential components, but the subjective experience and behavior are always rooted in God's presence. God has poured himself into his people. The life he gives is life-giving; and, as such, it must be either passed on or extinguished. This is the story of Anthony of Egypt and of the early martyrs—indeed, it is the story of all the saints. They participated in the divine nature; and, godlike, they gave their lives in love. "I appeal to you therefore, brethren, by the mercies of God, to present your bodies as a living sacrifice, holy and acceptable to God, which is your spiritual worship" (Rom 12:1).

Holiness, like the liturgy, begins with theophany, God's self-revelation, but leads to full covenantal communion, the mutual indwelling of God and man. "He who eats my flesh and drinks my blood abides in me, and I in him" (Jn 6:56).

The biblical Apocalypse is the great literary witness to this saint-making power of the sacramental liturgy. The life of Anthony corresponds to the literal sense, the historical truth, and the divine meaning of Revelation, and of the entire Bible. The word explicates the sacraments. The sacraments actualize the word. The net effect is saints, those who have ears to hear (Mt 13:9).

❧

Much work needs to be done. There are books to be written, studies to be undertaken, sermons to be preached, prayers to be raised, and ordinary lives to be lived. *Every* interpreter of scripture, then, has something to offer. Listen to the words of the Pontifical Biblical Commission, in its 1993 document *The Interpretation of the Bible in the Church*:

> *What characterizes Catholic exegesis is that it deliberately places itself within the living tradition of the church, whose first concern is fidelity to the revelation attested by the Bible. Modern hermeneutics has made clear, as we have noted, the impossibility of interpreting a text without starting from a "pre-understanding" of one type or another.*
>
> *Catholic exegetes approach the biblical text with a pre-understanding which holds closely together modern scientific culture and the religious tradition emanating from Israel and from the early Christian community. Their interpretation stands thereby in continuity with a dynamic pattern of interpre-*

*tation that is found within the Bible itself and continues in the
life of the church. This dynamic pattern corresponds to the re-
quirement that there be a lived affinity between the interpreter
and the object, an affinity which constitutes, in fact, one of the
conditions that makes the entire exegetical enterprise possible.*[12]

That lived affinity—that hermeneutical proximity—is
nothing less than holiness, and it is lived most surely in the
church's liturgy. A generation ago, Carroll Stuhlmueller anticipated the conclusions of the Biblical Commission as he
issued his own challenge to Catholic biblical studies: "By
studying sacred doctrine in the context of liturgical worship, the
Christian anticipates the direction and the contribution of
modern biblical scholarship. . . . If in the past Scripture had
been taught and read with a keen sense of its constant liturgical use in Israel and in the apostolic Church, then the discoveries of the contemporary scriptural movement would not
have taken Catholic theologians, religion teachers or Bible
readers by surprise. . . . For depth of understanding, then, we
must approach God's word in the liturgical spirit with which
it was composed."[13]

There is work to be done. But, if we are willing to take
up the work, we can be sure that we stand at the cusp of a
great new century for the study of the sacred page—from the
heart of the church.

This is no fanciful view from an ivory tower. Think of it,
instead, as a vision on an ivory pyx—that liturgical vessel
carved so many centuries ago by our Christian ancestors and

kept safe from invading marauders—that vessel of the eucharist etched with the altar, the Word, the lighted lamp, and the historical event: the empty tomb of Jesus Christ.

That vision has survived the tumultuous centuries. With a far greater permanence, economy, typology, and mystagogy have been etched into the church's memory, etched into Christian tradition.

ABBREVIATIONS

Ante-Nicene Fathers = ANF
Catechism of the Catholic Church = CCC
Enchiridion Biblicum = E.B.
Dei Verbum = DV
Sacrosanctum Concilium = SC
Summa Theologiae = S.Th.

NOTES

Note: In the case of patristic citations, I have often consulted multiple translations as well as the originals, whenever possible. Some quotations are new translations; some quotations are composites where I have exercised editorial judgment, drawing from varied translations. In all cases, I have tried to achieve maximum clarity and fidelity to the sense of the originals.

Introduction

1. One of the members of the Vatican II committee for the revision of the Lectionary, Adrien Nocent, commented: "Without a doubt, the massive introduction of Scripture in the missal constitutes the most spectacular renewal of the Church's liturgical reform." From "La parole de Dieu et Vatican II," in *Liturgia, Opera Divina e Umana,* ed. Pierre Jounel et al. (Rome: Edizioni liturgiche, 1982), p. 136; translated and cited by Normand Bonneau in *The Sunday Lectionary: Ritual Word, Paschal Shape* (Collegeville, Minn.: Liturgical Press, 1998), p. 3.

2. For a useful discussion of the meaning, kinds, and uses of lectionaries, see Bonneau, *Sunday Lectionary,* pp. 3–4: "First, a lectionary is not the Bible as such, but passages selected from the Bible. It is a product of one of the many ways a community appropriates the Bible for the purpose of worship. Second, the passages are not presented in a helter-skelter fashion but are selected and organized in patterns according to specific principles. Third, since the selected and ordered passages from scripture are to be used at public worship, the type and frequency of a community's public worship will greatly determine how passages are

chosen and distributed. These three aspects of a lectionary are always present and always mutually influencing each other. . . ." He further notes: "Since Vatican II, the word 'lectionary' evokes in the mind of Roman Catholics a large, ornate, and imposing book containing the scriptural passages proclaimed at the Eucharist. The *Lectionary for Mass* is in fact a collection of *six* different lectionaries, all sharing the common features of containing biblical passages selected to be read at eucharistic celebrations. Printed in one book or in several volumes, the *Lectionary for Mass* comprises a lectionary for Sundays and Solemnities (solemnities here means feasts of the Lord which do not usually occur or never fall on a Sunday, such as Christmas, Epiphany, the Easter Triduum, Ascension), a lectionary for weekday Masses, a lectionary for Masses on saints' days, a lectionary for ritual Masses (confirmation, marriage, funerals, etc.), a lectionary for Masses for various occasions (for the Church, for civil needs, etc.), and a lectionary for votive Masses."

3. Fritz West, *Scripture and Memory: The Ecumenical Hermeneutic of the Three-Year Lectionaries* (Collegeville, MN: Liturgical Press, 1997), p. 25.

4. West 27.

5. On the different patterns of scriptural readings in the eucharistic celebrations of other rites (e.g., Byzantine, Mozarabic, Ambrosian), see Michael Kunzler, *The Church's Liturgy* (New York: Continuum, 2001), pp. 214–15.

6. Pontifical Biblical Commission, *Interpretation of the Bible in the Church* (Boston: St. Paul, 1953), p. 52.

7. West 27.

Chapter 1

1. See Augustine of Hippo, *Confessions* 8.6.15.

2. Athanasius, *Life of Anthony* 2–3 .

3. Joseph Cardinal Ratzinger, quoted in *Biblical Interpretation in Crisis: The Ratzinger Conference on Bible and Church,* ed. Richard John Neuhaus, Encounter Series (Grand Rapids, MI: Eerdmans, 1989), p. 114.

4. Geoffrey Wainwright, "Tradition as Liturgical Act," in *The Quadrilog: Tradition and the Future of Ecumenism,* ed. George H. Tavard,

Kenneth Hagen, and Marc R. Alexander (Collegeville, MN: Liturgical Press, 1994), p. 140.

Chapter 2

1. Origen, *Homilies on Jeremiah* 18.4.

2. Stephen D. Benin, *The Footprints of God: Divine Accommodation in Jewish and Christian Thought* (Albany, NY: SUNY Press, 1993), p. 90.

3. Andrew Louth, *Discerning the Mystery: An Essay on the Nature of Theology* (Oxford: Clarendon, 1983), p. 3.

4. Jean Corbon, *The Wellspring of Worship*, trans. Matthew O'Connell (New York: Paulist Press, 1988), p. 6.

5. Christoph Schonborn, "The Divine Economy Interwoven through New Catechetical Work," O.P., in *Reflections on the Catechism of the Catholic Church,* ed. James P. Socias (Chicago: Midwest Theological Forum, 1993), p. 79.

6. *Ibid.* 79.

7. Corbon 6. The *purpose* of Christian liturgy, says I. H. Dalmais, O.P. is "to express man's faith in the divine economy and perpetuate the living effects of the incarnation." See *Introduction to the Liturgy,* trans. Roger Capel (Baltimore: Helicon, 1961), p. 27. See also Jean Danielou, S.J., "The Sacraments and the History of Salvation," in *Liturgy and the Word of God,* papers given at the Third National Congress of the Centre de Pastorale Liturgique (Collegeville, MN: Liturgical Press, 1959), pp. 21–32, at 29: "The object of faith is the existence of a divine plan."

8. Henri de Lubac, S.J., *Medieval Exegesis,* vol. 1 (Grand Rapids, MI: Eerdmans, 1998), p. 230.

9. There are many more examples. New creation: Is 40:12–28; 42:5–12; 54:9–10; 65:17; Jer 31:35–37; 33:19–20; Ezek 34:25–30. New exodus: Is 11:11–16; 40:3–5; Jer 16:14–16; 23:1–8; Ezek 20:32–44. New kingdom/Jerusalem/Zion: Is 2:1–4; 9:6–7; 11:1–10; 65:18; Jer 33:15–22; Ezek 34:11–31; 36:16–28; chs. 40–48. Moreover, Is 43:15–21 combines new creation and new exodus. Is 44:24–28 combines new creation and new Jerusalem. Jer 32:36–44 and Ezek 34:11–31 and 36:16–28 combine new exodus and new kingdom/Jerusalem. Is

45:7–20 and 51:1–16 and Jer 33:14–26 combine all three. Consider, too, that the Hebrew word *bara'* ("create") is used sixteen times in Is 40–55, where new exodus prophecy is most common.

10. Jean Danielou, S.J., *From Shadows to Reality: Studies in the Typology of the Fathers* (London: Burns and Oates, 1960), p. 157.

11. Jean Danielou, S.J., *The Lord of History,* trans. Nigel Abercrombie (New York: Meridian, 1968), p. 140. See also Augustine, *De Doctrina* 1.2 and Thomas Aquinas S.Th. I.i.10, in body of article and in Quodlibet IX.7.a.14.

12. Enrico Mazza, *Mystagogy: A Theology of Liturgy in the Patristic Age,* trans. Matthew J. O'Connell (New York: Pueblo, 1989), p. 11.

13. Jean Danielou, S.J., *The Bible and the Liturgy* (Notre Dame, Ind.: Notre Dame University Press, 1956), p. 5.

14. Danielou, *The Lord of History,* 140.

15. Gerhard von Rad, "Typological Interpretation of the Old Testament," in *Essays on Old Testament Hermeneutics,* ed. Claus Westermann (Richmond, VA: John Knox Press, 1964), p. 17.

16. Christopher J. H. Wright, *Knowing Jesus through the Old Testament* (Downers Grove, IL: InterVarsity Press, 1992), pp. 111–12.

17. Danielou, *The Bible and the Liturgy,* 5.

18. Mazza, *Mystagogy,* 2.

19. Robert Taft, "The Liturgy of the Great Church," *Dumbarton Oaks Papers,* nn. 34 and 35 (1980–81), p. 59.

20. *Reply to Faustus* 20.21.

21. And in the sacraments there occurs an analogous illumination of uncomprehending minds. Raymond Brown observes: "In John's stories, then, there is a constant double level of language. Those who talk to Jesus or about him speak of what is important to them on one level (earth), while Jesus tries to lead them to another, more important level of realities (heaven). By reading these stories to us in the liturgy, the Church reminds us that Jesus is still struggling to get us to see deeper realities." *Reading the Gospels with the Church* (Cincinnati, OH: St. Anthony Messenger Press, 1996), p. 35.

22. Danielou, *The Lord of History,* 259.

23. Jeremy Driscoll, O.S.B., *Theology at the Eucharistic Table* (Rome: Studia Anselmiana, 2003), p. 221.

24. John Breck, *The Power of the Word in the Worshiping Church* (Crestwood, NY: St. Vladimir's Seminary Press, 1986), p. 19, emphasis in original.

Chapter 3

1. James A. Sanders, *From Sacred Story to Sacred Text* (Philadelphia: Fortress, 1987), p. 162. See also William J. Abraham, *Canon and Criterion in Christian Theology* (Oxford: Clarendon Press, 1998), p. 413: "The canon of Scripture was simply a list of books to be read in worship and to be used for spiritual direction and instruction in the Church."

2. Eugene Maly, "Israel—God's Liturgical People," in *Liturgy for the People: Essays in Honor of Gerald Ellard, S.J.,* ed. William J. Leonard, S.J. (Milwaukee, WI: Bruce, 1963), pp. 10ff.

3. Maly 20.

4. Gordon J. Wenham, *Numbers: An Introduction and Commentary* (Downers Grove, IL: InterVarsity Press, 1981), p. 26.

5. Klaus Westermann, quoted in Maly, p. 13.

6. Wenham 26.

7. Wenham 29.

8. Maly 15.

9. William Riley, *King and Cultus in Chronicles: Worship and the Reinpretation of History* (Sheffield: Sheffield Academic Press, 1993), p. 156.

10. See Gerhard von Rad, *Wisdom in Israel* (London: SCM Press, 1993), pp. 186–89.

11. Eugene LaVerdiere, *The Eucharist in the New Testament and the Early Church* (Collegeville, MN: Liturgical Press, 1996), p. 54.

12. Raymond E. Brown, *New Testament Essays* (New York: Doubleday, 1968).

13. Raymond E. Brown, *An Introduction to the Gospel of John,* ed. Francis J. Moloney (New York: Doubleday, 2003), p. 230.

14. *Ibid.* 234. Brown adds: "Moreover, among the four Gospels it is to John most of all that we owe the deep Christian understanding of the purpose of baptism and the eucharist. It is John who tells us that through baptismal water God begets children unto himself and pours forth upon them his Spirit (3:5; 7:37–39). Thus baptism becomes a source of eternal life (4:13–14), and the eucharist is the necessary food of that life

(6:57). Finally, in a dramatic scene (19:34), John shows symbolically that both of these sacraments, baptismal water and eucharistic blood, have the source of their existence and power in the death of Jesus. This Johannine sacramentalism is neither merely antidocetic nor peripheral, but reflects the essential connection between the sacramental way of receiving life within the church at the end of the first century and the way in which life was offered to those who heard Jesus in Palestine."

15. Many Protestant commentators have discerned the influence of primitive liturgy on the formation of the New Testament. See, e.g., Gordon S. Wakefield, *The Liturgy of St. John* (London: Epworth, 1985); and Etienne Trocmé, *The Passion as Liturgy* (London: SCM Press, 1983).

16. John Koenig, *The Feast of the World's Redemption: Eucharistic Origins and Christian Mission* (Harrisburg, PA: Trinity Press International, 2000), pp. 136ff. See also "The Pauline Theology of Sacrifice," in Robert J. Daly, S.J., *Christian Sacrifice: The Judaeo-Christian Background Before Origen* (Washington, DC: Catholic University of America Press, 1978), pp. 230–60.

17. See Roch Kereszty, "The Eucharist in the Letter to the Hebrews," *Communio* 26 (1999): 154–67. See also Cheslyn Jones et al. (eds.), *The Study of Liturgy* (London: SPCK, 1992), pp. 201ff.

18. Maly 12.

19. Carroll Stuhlmueller, C.P., *Thirsting for the Lord: Essays in Biblical Spirituality* (Staten Island, NY: Alba House, 1977), p. 102.

20. Gerard Sloyan, "The Liturgical Proclamation of the Word of God," in *Bible, Life, and Worship: Twenty-Second North American Liturgical Week* (Washington, DC: The Liturgical Conference, 1961), p. 9.

21. Eugene Ulrich, "The Notion and Definition of Canon," in *The Canon Debate,* ed. Lee Martin McDonald and James A. Sanders (Peabody, MA: Hendrickson, 2002), p. 28.

22. Everett Ferguson, "Factors Leading to the Selection and Closure of the New Testament Canon," in McDonald and Sanders, p. 296.

23. P. J. Tomson, "The New Testament Canon as the Embodiment of Evolving Christian Attitudes Towards the Jews," in *Canonization and Decanonization,* ed. A Van Der Kooij and K. Van Der Toorn (Leiden: Brill, 1998), pp. 108–11. On early Judaism's distinctions between biblical and other authoritative sources of "oral law," see Benjamin D. Som-

mer, "Unity and Plurality in Jewish Canons: The Case of the Oral and Written Torahs," in *One Scripture or Many? Canon from Biblical, Theological and Philsophical Perspectives,* ed. C. Helmer and C. Landmesser (New York: Oxford University Press, 2004), pp. 130–31: "The Pentateuch is recited in the liturgy, in its entirety and following a set of very exact rules. Similarly, selections from the Nach [i.e., prophets] are also recited liturgically following specific rules. Rabbinic texts are not chanted in rabbinic liturgy in this manner. Further, the Pentateuch serves as a ritual object in a way that rabbinic texts do not. The scroll of the Pentateuch is carried about in formal procession during the synagogue service. . . . The common Jewish practice of reciting psalms is also ritual in nature."

24. Ferguson, "Factors Leading to the Selection," p. 296.

25. "The liturgy functions within the worshipping community as a mode of communication, and scriptural texts used in that context are, by definition, canonical." Harold P. Scanlin, "The Old Testament Canon in the Orthodox Churches," in *New Perspectives on Historical Theology: Essays in Memory of John Meyendorff,* ed. Bradley Nasef (Grand Rapids, MI: Eerdmans, 1996), p. 310.

26. Eusebius, *Ecclesiastical History* 6.12.2.

Chapter 4

1. Irenaeus, *Against Heresies* 1.10.3.

2. Walter Bruggemann, "The Covenanted Family," *Journal of Current Social Issues* 14 (1977): 18.

3. F. M. Cross, "Kinship and Covenant in Ancient Israel," in *From Epic to Canon: History and Literature in Ancient Israel* (Baltimore: Johns Hopkins University Press, 1998), p. 8.

4. Jacob Neusner, *Making God's Word Work* (New York: Continuum, 2004), pp. 232–33.

5. Baruch Levine, *Leviticus* (Philadelphia: Jewish Publication Society, 1989), pp. xxxviii, 11. See also *idem, In the Presence of the Lord* (Leiden: Brill, 1974), p. 38.

6. M. G. Kline, *By Oath Consigned: A Reinterpretation of the Covenant Signs of Circumcision and Baptism* (Grand Rapids, MI: Eerdmans, 1968), p. 28.

7. Kline 43.

8. Oswald Loretz, *The Truth of the Bible* (New York: Herder and Herder, 1968), pp. 97, 101.

9. Eusebius 3.25.1–7; see McDonald and Sanders, p. 432.

10. See Gunnar Ostborn, *Cult and Canon: A Study in the Canonization of the Old Testament* (Uppsala: Almqvist & Wiksells, 1950), pp. 75–96 (Ch. 4: "The Canon as a Representation Concerning Yahweh's Activity"). "Illustrative of the Canon's character of being a representation about Yahweh's works is furthermore the designation 'the Old Covenant,' or 'the writings of the Old Covenant,' used with reference to the Canon. As indicated above, this designation is an adequate expression of what the Canon really is. At the same time, this designation bears witness to the fact that there was a definite comprehensive view concerning the Canonical writings. As a prerequisite of correctly understanding this designation, however, it is necessary to take the concept Covenant as meaning not only a social condition regulated by laws, but a new and good order brought about by Yahweh" (p. 76). "It appears to have been a general custom among the early Christians to designate the Biblical writings as books of the two Covenants. We find such a designation in Athanasius . . . as well as in Amphilochius. . . . This linguistic usage, which in all probability originates from the OT expression 'the Book of the Covenant' . . . in Ex. xxiv. 7 and 2 K. xxiii. 2, depends, of course, on the essential contents of the writings in question, i.e., their fundamental idea. It is to be seen in the Church Fathers that this is really the case. . . . Thus we have arrived at the result that, from the viewpoint of its contents, the Canon is primarily to be regarded as a 'Book of the Covenant.' The religion of Israel is, like that of the Christians, a religion of a covenant. Hence the concept covenant comprises such a comprehensive view of the OT writings as we have earlier claimed to be a characteristic of their canonicity. Accordingly, it may be said that *the notion of the Covenant in the Biblical writings constitutes the fundamental condition of their canonization*" (p. 77, emphasis added).

11. "The Bible, we might say, is at home in the Church and receives the treatment accorded to a member of the household." Michael Leahy, "The Guardian of the Word—the Church," in *The Word of Life: Essays on the Bible* (Westminster, MD: Newman Press, 1960), p. 21.

12.1 Enoch 69:15–27; see J. H. Charlesworth (ed.), *The Old Tes-*

tament Pseudepigrapha: Apocalyptic Literature and Testaments (New York: Doubleday, 1983), pp. 47–49.

13. *Sifre Deut.* 330.

14. Robert Murray, S.J., *The Cosmic Covenant: Biblical Themes of Justice, Peace and the Integrity of Creation* (London: Sheed & Ward, 1992), pp. 7–13; Margaret Barker, *The Lost Prophet: The Book of Enoch and Its Influence on Christianity* (Nashville, TN: Abingdon, 1988); *idem,* "The Book of Enoch and Cosmic Sin," *The Ecologist* (January/February 2000): 30ff. See Roland de Vaux, *Ancient Israel: Its Life and Institutions,* vol. 2 (New York: McGraw-Hill, 1961), p. 481: "Creation is the first action in the history of salvation; once it was over, God stopped work, and he was then able to make a covenant. . . . The 'sign' of the Covenant made at the dawn of creation is the observance of the sabbath." See also R. Elior, *The Three Temples: On the Emergence of Jewish Mysticism* (Oxford: Littman Library, 2004), p. 140.

15. See also CCC 346.

16. *Dies Domini* 8; CCC 288, 346.

17. For a similar but distinct approach to "re-templing," or "templization," see Daniel S. Ben Ezra, *The Impact of Yom Kippur on Early Christianity* (Tubingen: Mohr Siebeck, 2003), pp. 269–72, where he traces the "the long-term process of *templization*" from ancient Israel into the early Christian tradition.

18. *Midrash Tehillim.* Edition Buder, 1[2], p. 3.

19. Hippolytus, ANF 5, pp. 170–72.

20. Harvey H. Guthrie, Jr., *Theology as Thanksgiving* (New York: Seabury, 1981); Hartmut Gese, "The Origin of the Lord's Supper," in *Essays on Biblical Theology* (Minneapolis, MN: Augsburg Publishing House, 1981).

21. Gese 131.

22. Tim Gray, "From Jewish Passover to Christian Eucharist: The Todah Sacrifice as Backdrop for the Last Supper," in *Catholic for a Reason III: Scripture and the Mystery of the Mass,* ed. Scott Hahn and Regis Flaherty (Steubenville, OH: Emmaus Road, 2004), p. 72.

23. Jean LaPorte, *Eucharistia in Philo* (New York: Edwin Mellen, 1983), p. 24.

24. *Pesiqta,* quoted in Gese 133.

25. Pliny the Younger, *Letters,* X.96–97. For an online version of this text, see: http://ccat.sas.upenn.edu/jod/texts/pliny.html.

26. On Tertullian's covenantal understanding and use of *sacramentum,* see D. Michaelides, *Sacramentum Chez Tertullien* (Paris: Etudes Augustiniennes, 1970).

27. See A. G. Martimort (ed.), *The Church at Prayer* (Collegeville, MN: Liturgical Press, 1992), I:255–56.

28. Marvin W. Meyer (ed.), *The Ancient Mysteries: A Sourcebook of Sacred Texts* (Philadelphia: University of Pennsylvania, 1987), pp. 199ff.

29. Quoted in Meyer 251–52.

30. Segal 4.

31. Wright 260, 262.

32. Segal 11.

33. Segal 12.

34. Dom Anscar Vonier, O.S.B., *The New and Eternal Covenant* (New York: Benziger Brothers, 1930), p. 15.

35. Romano Guardini, *Meditations before Mass* (Manchester, NH: Sophia Institute Press, 1993), p. 191.

Chapter 5

1. Around 322 A.D., the emperor Constantine, in an effort to unify worship in Constantinople, directed that scribes copy out fifty complete books of the scriptures and distribute them to the churches. These were "elaborately bound," Eusebius tells us *(Life of Constantine* 4.36–37).

2. Athanasius, *Letter to Marcellinus,* 11.

3. Theodore of Mopsuestia, *Commentary on the Twelve Prophets,* trans. Robert C. Hill (Washington, DC: Catholic University of America Press, 2004), p. 289; cf. Chrysostom, *First Homily on David and Saul.*

4. Augustine, *Confessions* 8.12.

5. Augustine, *Confessions* 5.9.

6. See W. Harrington, *The Path of Biblical Theology* (Dublin: Gill and Macmillan, 1973), p. 329: "Larcher would consider the liturgy as a privileged context for a Christian actualisation of the Old Testament. It is in this setting that Scripture regains its sacred dimension and that the saving events of salvation recorded in the Old Testament spring to life again. Christ has brought the two Testaments together; this unity is con-

secrated by the liturgical celebration of his mystery in the Church's cult. For, in the context of the great mysteries of the life of Christ, Scripture becomes again a living and actual word—but now in the sense in which Jesus fulfilled it, in a total reference to him, to what he did and taught."

7. Kline 141.

8. Augustin Bea, *The Word of God and Mankind,* trans. Dorothy White (Chicago: Franciscan Herald Press, 1967), pp. 178–80.

9. "Scripture indeed becomes faith's normative object in its liturgical use or when the reading or study of Scripture otherwise becomes living proclamation or adoration. When Scripture appears in such power, its authority is that of proclamation and sacrament and prayer generally: it is the authority of God's own presence in his word, to create and nurture faith. And it is a chief aspect of the church's canonizing dogma . . . that the particular books gathered in the Bible are so to be privileged liturgically, homiletically, and devotionally that these books may be constants of proclamation and prayer." Robert W. Jenson, *Systematic Theology,* vol. 1 (New York: Oxford University Press, 1997), p. 28.

10. Augustine, cited in Karl Hermann Schelkle, "Sacred Scripture and Word of God," in *Dogmatic vs. Biblical Theology,* ed. Herbert Vorgrimler (London: Burns and Oates, 1964), pp. 11–30.

11. See Lucien Deiss, C.S.Sp., *God's Word and God's People,* trans. Matthew J. O'Connell (Collegeville, MN: Liturgical Press, 1976), pp. 256–257, and F. X. Durrwell, *FX Durrwell C.Ss.R.,* Theologians Today series (London: Sheed and Ward), 1972), pp. 62–65.

12. Martimort I:247.

13. *Divino Afflante Spiritu* 37.

14. Dei Verbum cites Pope Leo XIII in *Providentissimus Deus,* E.B. 125, which reads, in part: "For all the books which the Church receives as sacred and canonical are written wholly and entirely with all their parts, at the dictation of the Holy Spirit; and so far is it from being possible that any error can coexist with inspiration, that inspiration not only is essentially incompatible with error, but excludes and rejects it as absolutely and necessarily as it is impossible that God Himself, the supreme Truth, can utter that which is not true. This is the ancient and unchanging faith of the Church. . . ." Noteworthy is the statement in the immediately preceding paragraph: "But it is absolutely wrong and forbidden

either to narrow inspiration to certain parts only of Holy Scripture or to admit that the sacred writer has erred. As to the system of those who, in order to rid themselves of these difficulties, do not hesitate to concede that divine inspiration regards the things of faith and morals, and nothing beyond . . . this system cannot be tolerated" (E.B. 124). Dei Verbum also cites *Divino Afflante Spiritu* on two significant points:

1) On the Thomist distinction between principal and instrumental authorship (art. 11, n. 2), precisely at the point where Pope Pius XII gives a ringing endorsement of St. Thomas's explanatory theory of instrumentality to explain the mystery of concurrence in the dual authorship of Scripture: "Among these it is worthy of special mention that Catholic theologians, following the teaching of the Holy Fathers and especially of the Angelic and Common Doctor, have examined and explained the nature and effects of biblical inspiration more exactly and more fully than was wont to be done in previous ages. For having begun by expounding minutely the principle that the inspired writer, in composing the sacred book, is the living and reasonable instrument of the Holy Spirit, they rightly observe that, impelled by the divine motion, he so uses his faculties and powers, that from the book composed by him all may easily infer 'the special character of each one and, as it were, his personal traits' (art. 33, E.B. 556)."

2) On the nature and extent of inerrancy and the authority of Leo XIII's teaching in *Providentissimus Deus* (art. 11, n. 5). Here we have very strong statements of Pius XII's solemn endorsement of Leo XIII's teaching on this controversial subject: "When, subsequently, some Catholic writers, in spite of this solemn definition of Catholic doctrine, by which such divine authority is claimed for the 'entire books with all their parts' as to secure freedom from any error whatsoever, ventured to restrict the truth of Sacred Scripture solely to matters of faith and morals, and to regard other matters whether in the domain of physical science or history, as 'obiter dicta' and—as they contended—in no wise connected with faith, Our Predecessor of immortal memory, Leo XIII in the Encyclical Letter, *Providentissimus Deus,* published on November 18th in the year 1893, justly and rightly condemned these errors and safe-guarded the studies of the Divine Books by most wise precepts and rules" (art. 1, E.B. 538). He refers to Leo XIII's encyclical as "the supreme guide in biblical

studies" which he resolves to commemorate for the purpose of safe-guarding scripture studies which "may most opportunely be done by ratifying and inculcating all that was wisely laid down by Our Predecessor and ordained by His successors for the consolidating and perfecting of the work . . ." (art. 2, E.B. 538).

Then Pius XII underscores the primary concern: "The first and greatest care of Leo XIII was to set forth the teaching on the truth of the Sacred Books and to defend it from attack. Hence with grave words did he proclaim that there is no error whatsoever if the sacred writer, speaking of things of the physical order 'went by what sensibly appeared' as the Angelic Doctor says, speaking either 'in figurative language, or in terms which were commonly used at the time, and which in many instances are in daily use at this day, even among the most eminent men of science.' For 'sacred writers, or to speak more accurately—the words are St. Augustine's—the Holy Ghost, Who spoke by them, did not intend to teach men these things—that is the essential nature of the things of the universe—things in no way profitable to salvation: which principle will apply to cognate sciences, and especially to history,' that is, by refuting, 'in a somewhat similar way the fallacies of the adversaries and defending the historical truth of Sacred Scripture from their attacks.' Nor is the sacred writer to be taxed with error, if 'copyists have made mistakes in the text of the Bible,' or, 'if the real meaning of a passage remains ambiguous.' Finally, it is absolutely wrong and forbidden 'either to narrow inspiration to certain passages of Holy Scripture, or to admit that the sacred writer has erred,' since divine inspiration 'not only is essentially incompatible with error but excludes and rejects it as absolutely and necessarily as it is impossible that God Himself, the supreme Truth, can utter that which is not true. This is the ancient and constant faith of the Church' " (art. 3, E.B. 539).

Pius XII concludes his purpose statement by clarifying the authority of Leo XIII's teaching: "This teaching, which Our Predecessor Leo XIII set forth with such solemnity, We also proclaim with Our authority and We urge all to adhere to it religiously. No less earnestly do We inculcate obedience at the present day to the counsels and exhortations which he, in his day, so wisely enjoined" (art. 4, E.B. 540).

15. *Providentissimus Deus* 20.

16. *1 Clement* 45.

17. William Jurgens has indexed many patristic texts supporting the thesis "No error can be found in the Sacred Scriptures." See his *Faith of the Early Fathers,* vol. 1 (Collegeville, MN: Liturgical Press, 1970), p. 413.

18. Augustine, *Letters* 82.1.3.

19. Martimort II:65.

20. Germanus of Constantinople, *Exegesis* 24, quoted in Martimort II:60.

21. See, e.g., the description of Ephesus by John Anthony McGuckin in *St. Cyril of Alexandria and the Christological Controversy* (Crestwood, NY: St. Vladimir's Seminary Press, 2004), p. 77.

22. Origen, *On Exodus* 13.3.

23. See Francis J. Schaefer, "The Tabernacle: Its History, Structure and Custody," in *The Ecclesiastical Review* (May 1935): 449–68. See also C. P. Bowler, *Living the Truth* (Sydney, Australia: FSM, 2004), p. 198: "In 380, Catholicism was recognised as the official religion of the Empire. So the Bible could again be freely used; and it became a powerful influence in the education of the people. The Emperor Theodosius, for instance, ordered it to be displayed in every court of justice in his vast domain. And at the Council of Constantinople held in 381, it was placed on the throne to indicate that the word of God which it contains was presiding over the Assembly. Paulinus tells us that, in the fourth century, every Tabernacle had two compartments—one for the Eucharist, and another for the Bible, since each is, in its own way, the supernatural food of our souls."

24. Massey H. Shepherd, Jr., *The Worship of the Church* (Greenwich, CT: Seabury Press, 1952), p. 4.

25. Driscoll 165.

26. Driscoll 103.

Chapter 6

1. Nahum N. Glatzer (ed.), *The Passover Haggadah* (New York: Schocken, 1989), p. 29.

2. Kline 34.

3. Glatzer viii.

4. Max Thurian, *The Eucharistic Memorial,* trans. J. G. Davies (Richmond, VA: John Knox Press, 1962), p. 18; cf. Fritz Chenderlin, *"Do This as My Memorial"* (Rome: Biblical Institute Press, 1982).

5. Robert Louis Wilken, *The Spirit of Early Christian Thought: Seeking the Face of God* (New Haven, CT: Yale University Press, 2003), p. 34.

6. Thurian, *The Eucharistic Memorial*, 20ff, emphases in original.

7. Rosario F. Esposito (ed.), *Carissimi in San Paolo: Lettere, Articoli, Opuscoli, Scritti Inediti di Don Giaccomo Alberione dal 1933 al 1969* (Rome: Edizioni Paoline, 1971).

8. Dom Cyprian Vagaggini, O.S.B., *Theological Dimensions of the Liturgy,* trans. Leonard J. Doyle and W. A. Jurgens (Collegeville, MN: Liturgical Press, 1976), p. 483.

9. Glatzer 35.

10. Cf. *Mishnah Pesachim* 10.5.

11. Thurian, *The Eucharistic Memorial*, 33.

12. Jean Danielou, S.J., "The Sacraments in the History of Salvation," in *The Liturgy and the Word of God* (Collegeville, MN: Liturgical Press, 1959), p. 28, emphasis added.

13. Sofia Cavalletti, "Memorial and Typology in Jewish and Christian Liturgy," in *Letter and Spirit Vol. 1: Reading Salvation: Word, Worship, and the Mysteries,* ed. Scott W. Hahn (Steubenville, OH: Emmaus Road, 2005), pp. 69–86.

14. Wilken, *The Spirit of Early Christian Thought,* 35.

15. Segal 12, 17.

16. Segal 89.

17. Augustine, in Thomas Spidlík (ed.), *Drinking from the Hidden Fountain: A Patristic Breviary,* trans. Paul Drake (Kalamazoo, MI: Cistercian Publications, 1994), p. 338.

18. Schmemann 47–48.

19. Thurian, *The Eucharistic Memorial*, 31.

20. Thurian, *The Eucharistic Memorial*, 28.

21. W. H. Auden, "In Memory of W. B. Yeats," in *Poetry Past and Present,* ed. Frank Brady and Martin Price (New York: HBJ, 1974), p. 385.

22. Schmemann 85.

23. Pontifical Biblical Commission, *The Interpretation of the Bible in the Church* (Boston: *St. Paul*, 1993), 124.

24. *Rosarium Mariae Virginis* 13; see also *Mediator Dei* 165.

25. Cavalletti, "Memorial and Typology," 69–86.

26. Robin Darling Young, *In Procession Before the World: Martyrdom*

NOTES

as Public Liturgy in Early Christianity (Milwaukee, WI: Marquette University Press, 2001).

27. See Ignatius, *Romans* 4, in *The Apostolic Fathers,* ed. J. B. Lightfoot and J. R. Harmer (London: Macmillan, 1891), p. 151.

28. See *Martyrdom of Polycarp* 14–15 in Lightfoot and Harmer 207–8.

Chapter 7

1. It is interesting to note, with F. X. Durrwell, that "Scripture speaks only of the 'coming' of Christ; it ignores any mention whatsoever of a 'return.'" Durrwell, F.-X., *Eucharist, Presence of Christ* (Denville, NJ: Dimension, 1974), p. 18. The word *parousia* occurs in only one place in the gospels, in Matthew 24, and there it does not mean "second coming" (a term that occurs nowhere in the Bible).

2. Alfred Loisy, *The Gospel and the Church* (Philadelphia: Fortress Press, 1976), p. 166.

3. Pelikan I:124; see also David Edward Aune's *The Cultic Setting of Realized Eschatology in Early Christianity* (Leiden: Brill, 1972): "In the Apocalypse of John . . . the final judgment is realized in present experience within the context of worship" (p. 14). "Some of the references to the 'seeing' and 'coming' of Jesus within these Discourses apparently refer to the cultic vision or epiphany of the exalted Jesus, in which the actual pneumatic experience of a cultic Christophany is clothed in the language and imagery of coventional theophanic and Parousia Traditions" (p. 15). "The cultic worship of the Johannine community provided a present experience of the exalted and living Jesus in terms of the recurring actualization of his future Parousia. This recurring culting 'coming' of the exalted Jesus was conceptualized in terms of traditional Christian Parousia imagery, and was directly experienced by the worshipping congregation 'in the Spirit,' or alternately as a presence mediated through the office of prophetic personalities" (pp. 101–2). "[T]he 'coming' of Jesus in the relevant passages under discussion from John 14 refers primarily to the recurring cultic 'coming' of Jesus in the form of a pneumatic or prophetic *visio Christi* within the setting of worship 'in the Spirit' as celebrated by the Johannine community. The eucharist undoubtedly forms the central moment of this setting within the cultic

worship of the community which the exalted Jesus, now present in Parousia splendor, pronounces both blessing and woe, salvation and judgment through prophetic cult personnel" (p. 129).

4. Pelikan I:126–27.

5. Dom Gregory Dix, *The Shape of the Liturgy* (New York: Seabury, 1982), pp. 252–53.

6. Liturgy of St. James, ANF 7, p. 540.

7. Baby Varghese, *West Syrian Liturgical Theology* (Burlington, VT: Ashgate, 2004), p. 83.

8. John Wordsworth (ed.), *Bishop Sarapion's Prayer Book: An Egyptian Pontifical Dated Probably About AD 350–356* (London: SPCK, 1899), p. 61.

9. For an excellent discussion of these and similar passages, see Jerome Gassner, O.S.B., *The Canon of the Mass* (New York: Herder, 1950), p. 158.

10. See Brian E. Daley, *The Hope of the Early Church: A Handbook of Patristic Eschatology* (Peabody, MA: Hendrickson, 2003), pp. 12–13.

11. Segal 87–89.

12. Martimort I:248.

13. Erik Peterson, *The Angels and the Liturgy* (New York: Herder and Herder, 1962), p. ix.

14. Levine, *Leviticus* 216–17.

15. Eusebius, *Ecclesiastical History* 5.24.3. See also W. H. C. Frend, *The Rise of Christianity* (Philadelphia: Fortress Press, 1984), p. 127.

16. See, e.g., *Didache* 14; Ignatius, *Philadelphians* 4; Justin, *Dialogue* 117.

17. Ignatius of Antioch, *Magnesians* 6.1.

18. Erik Peterson brings this out in his extended study of the angels and the liturgy. Danielou and Wilken have also treated the subject at length. See Danielou, *The Angels and Their Mission*; Wilken, "Angels and Archangels: The Worship of Heaven and Earth," in *Antiphon* 6:1.

19. Joseph Ratzinger, *Eschatology* (Washington, DC: Catholic University of America Press, 1988), p. 203.

20. *Liber Graduum* 12.2–3. *The Book of Steps: The Syriac Liber Graduum,* trans. Robert A. Kitchen and Martien F. G. Parmentier (Kalamazoo, MI: Cistercian Publications, 2004), pp. 120–22.

21. Ignatius of Antioch, *Smyrnaeans* 7. In regard to divine punishment, Christoph Schonborn observes: "God's punishment is salutary.

No man is abandoned by God to his fallen nature. The punishment of being scattered, the *diaspora* of the nations, is also *a way of being healed, the possibility of being made holy.* God's original plan to make mankind his family now makes use of the solidarity of peoples and languages, of nations and races, *to prepare for his Church.*" In *Loving the Church: Spiritual Exercises Preached in the Presence of Pope John Paul II,* trans. John Saward (San Francisco: Ignatius Press, 1998), p. 85, emphases in original.

22. Wordsworth 63.

23. Ignatius of Antioch, *Ephesians* 20.2.

24. Irenaeus, *Against Heresies* 4.18.5.

25. SC 7.

26. Pierre Jounel, "The Bible in the Liturgy," in *The Liturgy and the Word of God,* p. 17.

27. Josef Jungmann, S.J., *Announcing the Word of God,* trans. Ronald Walls (New York: Herder and Herder, 1967), p. 160.

28. Origen, *Homilies on Numbers* 16.9, quoted in Olivier Clement, *The Roots of Christian Mysticism,* trans. Theodore Berkeley (London: New City Press, 1995), p. 97.

29. Schmemann, "Fast and Liturgy," *St. Vladimir's Theological Quarterly* 3:1 (1959): 2–9.

Chapter 8

1. On the similarities between Catholic and Jewish notions of tradition, see Benjamin D. Sommer, "Unity and Plurality in Jewish Canons: The Case of the Oral and Written Torahs," in *One Scripture or Many? Canon from Biblical, Theological and Philosophical Perspectives,* ed. C. Helmer and C. Landmesser (New York: Oxford University Press, 2004), p. 111. He also writes: "the shared emphasis in Jewish and Catholic thought on the continuity between scripture and tradition is noteworthy; and the implications of this continuity for biblical theology demand attention." He also writes: ". . . this examination bolsters the category of tradition as one that functions alongside scripture, or even as a category that encompasses scripture. Thus this study evinces the affinity between Catholic and Jewish approaches to the Bible. Catholic and Jewish scholars face remarkably similar tools and opportunities as they attempt to relate their scriptures, respectively, to the teachings of the magisterium and

to the apprehensions of *kelal Israel* (the community of Israel, or as it has been felicitously rendered, catholic Israel). For both groups of interpreters, the tension between scripture and tradition recedes, because for both groups the boundary separating scripture and tradition is subordinate to an overarching unity" (p. 109).

2. DV 9; CCC 80.

3. St. Basil, *On the Holy Spirit* 27, 66.

4. W. Robertson Nicoll, *The Expositor's Greek Testament,* vol. 2 (London: Hodder and Stoughton), 1912, p. 881.

5. Augustine, Sermon 267.4. See also CCC 809.

6. Augustine, *De Trinitate.*

7. CCC 1103.

8. Varghese 79, 82.

9. CCC 1099.

10. Pius XI, private audience, cited in Vagaggini 512.

11. Irenaeus, *Against Heresies* 4.18.5, cited in CCC 1327.

12. Prosper of Aquitaine, Letter 8, cited in CCC 1327.

13. CCC 1124.

14. John Henry Cardinal Newman, *An Essay on the Development of Christian Doctrine* (New York: Doubleday, 1960).

15. Yves M.-J. Congar, O.P., *Tradition and Traditions,* trans. Michael Naseby and Thomas Rainborough (New York: MacMillan, 1966), p. 434; italics in original.

16. Congar 429.

17. John Allen, "The Word from Rome," *National Catholic Reporter,* June 6, 2003, www.nationalcatholicreporter.org/word/archives.htm.

18. Hughes Oliphant Old, *The Reading and Preaching of the Scriptures in the Worship of the Christian Church,* vol. 1 (Grand Rapids, MI: Eerdmans, 1998), p. 100.

19. See also R. Elior, *The Three Temples: On the Emergence of Jewish Mysticism* (Oxford: Littman Library, 2004), p. 141: "The Covenant depended on oath and remembrance, knowledge and testimony—remembering the Covenant and observing its proper time in the cultic calendar, re-establishing the Covenant through sacrifices and offerings brought at a set time, Shavuot, and renewing the oath of the Covenant

or its finalization; such were the tasks of those with whom the divine Covenant was concluded."

20. Pius XI, *Quas Primas* 82–83.

21. Max Thurian, *Visible Unity and Tradition* (London: Darton, Longman, and Todd, 1964), p. 96.

22. *1 Clement* 5; Irenaeus, *Against Heresies* 3.3.4.

23. R. M. Grant quoted in Karlfried Froehlich, *Biblical Interpretation in the Early Church* (Philadelphia: Fortress Press, 1984), p. 14.

24. Irenaeus, *Against Heresies* 4.26.2, quoted in Froehlich 45.

25. *Smyrnaeans* 8.

26. Dom Prosper Gueranger, quoted in Yves M.-J. Congar, O.P., *The Meaning of Tradition,* trans. A. N. Woodrow (New York: Hawthorn, 1964), p. 125.

27. Cardinal Joseph Ratzinger, *Church, Ecumenism and Politics* (New York: Crossroad, 1988), p. 80.

28. Bertrand de Margerie, S.J., *The Greek Fathers: A History of Exegesis,* trans. Leonard Maluf (Petersham, MA: St. Bede's, 1993), p. 130.

29. Stanley Hauerwas, *Unleashing the Scripture: Freeing the Bible from Captivity to America* (Nashville: Abingdon, 1993), p. 27. Similarly, the Lutheran scholar Robert W. Jenson has written: "If we allow no final authority to churchly dogma, or to the organs by which the church can enunciate dogma, there can be no canon of Scripture. The slogan *sola scriptura,* if by that is meant 'apart from the creed, teaching office, or authoritative liturgy,' is an oxymoron." Robert W. Jenson, *Systematic Theology,* vol. 1 (New York: Oxford University Press, 1997), pp. 27–28.

30. Hauerwas 26.

31. Manlio Simonetti, *Biblical Interpretation in the Early Church,* trans. John A. Hughes (Edinburgh: T&T Clark, 1994), p. 1.

32. Congar, *Tradition and Traditions,* 448.

Chapter 9

1. Martimort I:248.

2. Martimort I:247.

3. Martimort I:248.

4. For Luther on Revelation, see Roland Bainton, *Here I Stand: A Life of Martin Luther* (New York: Mentor, 1950), p. 261.

5. Congar, *Tradition and Traditions,* 431.

6. Scott Hahn, *The Lamb's Supper* (New York: Doubleday, 1999), pp. 119–20.

7. Leonard L. Thompson, *The Book of Revelation: Apocalypse and Empire* (New York: Oxford University Press, 1990), pp. 72–73. Scholars as varied as Geoffrey Wainwright, David Aune, Ian Boxall, and Margaret Barker come to remarkably similar conclusions regarding the relationship of Apocalypse to liturgy. See Wainwright, *Eucharist and Eschatology* (New York: Oxford University Press, 1981), pp. 75–76; Aune, *The Cultic Setting of Realized Eschatology in Early Christianity* (Leiden: Brill, 1972), pp. 14–15, 101–2; Boxall, *Revelation: Vision and Insight* (London: SPCK, 2002), 150ff; Barker, "Parousia and Liturgy" in *The Revelation of Jesus Christ* (Edinburgh: T&T Clark, 2000), pp. 373ff.

8. Boxall 151.

9. See also *Ecclesia de Eucharistia* 19.

10. See Pauli Maniyattu, *Heaven on Earth: The Theology of Liturgical Space-Time in the East Syrian Curbana* (Rome: Mar Thoma Yogam, 1995). For Western applications, see Martimort I:198–99, 205.

11. Martimort I:248.

12. G. K. Beale, *1–2 Thessalonians* (Downers Grove, IL: InterVarsity Press, 2003), p. 138.

13. *Roman Missal,* Preface for Sundays in Ordinary Time V.

14. *Orientale Lumen* 11.

15. M. L. McClure, and C. L. Feltoe (ed. and trans.), *The Pilgrimage of Etheria* (London: SPCK, 1919), 94.

Chapter 10

1. Danielou, *Bible and the Liturgy* 130; Mazza, *Mystagogy,* 66ff.

2. Quoted in Mazza, *Mystagogy,* 91.

3. See Book Six of Hugh of St. Victor, *The Didascalicon of Hugh of St. Victor: A Medieval Guide to the Arts,* trans. Jerome Taylor (New York: Columbia University Press, 1961), pp. 135–51. Also see Grover A. Zinn, Jr., *"Historia fundamentum est:* The Role of History in the Contemplative Life According to Hugh of St. Victor," in *Contemporary Reflections on the Medieval Christian Tradition,* ed. George H. Shriver (Durham, NC: Duke University Press, 1964), pp. 135–58.

4. Thomas Aquinas, S.Th. I:1, 10, ad 1.

5. CCC 119, see also *Dei Verbum* 12.

6. Deiss 262.

7. Jacob Milgrom, *Leviticus 17–22: A New Translation with Introduction and Commentary,* Anchor Bible, vol. 3A (New York: Doubleday, 1991), p. 42.

8. Milgrom, quoted in Thomas B. Dozeman, "The Holiness of God in Contemporary Jewish and Christian Biblical Theology," in *God's Word for Our World,* vol. 2, ed. Harold J. Ellens et al. (London: T&T Clark, 2004), pp. 31–32.

9. Levine, *Leviticus* 216–17.

10. Jerome, *Letter* 114.2.

11. *Didascalia Apostolorum* 9.

12. Pontifical Biblical Commission, *Interpretation of the Bible in the Church* IV.c.1. Geoffrey Wainwright made the same point eloquently in his book *Doxology: The Praise of God in Doctrine and Life* (New York: Oxford University Press, 1980), pp. 175–76. It merits quotation at length:

"The way in which the liturgy acts as a hermeneutical continuum for the scriptures should be pretty clear by now, but five new or reformulated points may be made briefly here.

"First: the liturgy has contributed in the most concrete way to the preservation and transmission of the biblical text. Until the invention of printing, it was largely in order to meet liturgical needs that manuscripts were copied.

"Second: liturgical use sets the proper atmosphere for the exegete and interpreter. The fundamental motivation of Christian exegesis and hermeneutics should be doxological.

"Third: the liturgy also supplies thematic guidelines for the exegete and interpreter. It composes the multiple motifs of the scriptures into a coherent vision.

"Fourth: the liturgy is the pre-eminent place in which the Church ponders and applies the scriptures. . . .

"Fifth: some contemporary biblical scholars have recognized the contribution which the liturgy can make to surmounting the historico-cultural gulf between the ancient writings and the present community."

13. Stuhlmueller 103, emphasis added.

WORKS CONSULTED

Abraham, William J. *Canon and Criterion in Christian Theology.* Oxford: Clarendon Press, 1998.

Alexander, T. Desmond, and Simon Gathercole, eds. *Heaven on Earth: The Temple in Biblical Theology.* Carlisle, England: Paternoster Press, 2004.

Allert, Craig D. *Revelation, Truth, Canon and Interpretation: Studies in Justin Martyr's* Dialogue with Trypho. Leiden: Brill, 2002.

Allison, Dale C. *The New Moses: A Matthean Typology.* Minneapolis, MN: Augsburg Fortress, 1993.

Ambrose of Milan. *St. Ambrose on the Sacraments and on the Mysteries.* London: SPCK, 1950.

Anderson, E. Byron. *Worship and Christian Identity: Practicing Ourselves.* Collegeville, MN: Liturgical Press, 2003.

Anonymous. *The Book of Steps: The Syriac.* Kalamazoo, MI: Cistercian Publications, 2004.

Assisi Congress. *The Assisi Papers: Proceedings of the First International Congress of Pastoral Liturgy.* Collegeville, MN: Liturgical Press, 1957.

Athanasius. *The Life of Antony and the Letter to Marcellinus.* New York: Paulist Press, 1980.

———. *The Resurrection Letters.* Nashville, TN: Thomas Nelson Publishers, 1979.

Atkins, Peter. *Memory and Liturgy: The Place of Memory in the Composition and Practice of Liturgy.* Brookfield, VT: Ashgate Publishing Company, 2004.

Auerbach, Erich. *Mimesis: The Representation of Reality in Western Literature.* Princeton, NJ: Princeton University Press, 1953.

Augustine. *Confessions.* New York: Penguin, 1961.

———. *On Christian Doctrine.* Indianapolis, IN: Bobbs-Merrill, 1958.

———. *Sermons.* New Rochelle, NY: New City Press, 1992–93.

Aune, David. *The Cultic Setting of Realized Eschatology in Early Christianity.* Leiden: Brill, 1972.

Barker, Margaret. *The Great High Priest: The Temple Roots of Christian Liturgy.* London: T. & T. Clark, 2003.

Barrois, George A. *Jesus Christ and the Temple.* New York: St. Vladimir's Seminary Press, 1980.

Bartholomew, Craig G., and Michael W. Goheen. *The Drama of Scripture: Finding Our Place in the Biblical Story.* Grand Rapids, MI: Baker Academic, 2004.

Bartholomew, Craig, Colin Greene, and Karl Moller, eds. *After Pentecost: Language & Biblical Interpretation.* Grand Rapids, MI: Zondervan, 2001.

Bartholomew, Craig, C. Stephen Evans, Mary Healy, and Murray Rae, eds. *Behind the Text: History and Biblical Interpretation.* Grand Rapids, MI: Zondervan, 2003.

Bartholomew, Craig, Mary Healy, Karl Moller, and Robin Parry, eds. *Out of Egypt: Biblical Theology and Biblical Interpretation.* Grand Rapids, MI: Zondervan, 2004.

Barton, John, and Michael Wolter. *The Unity of Scripture and the Diversity of Canon.* Berlin: Walter de Gruyter, 2003.

Bea, Augustin. *The Word of God and Mankind.* Chicago: Franciscan Herald Press, 1967.

Beale, G. K. *1–2 Thessalonians.* Downers Grove, IL: InterVarsity Press, 2003.

———. *The Temple and the Church's Mission: A Biblical Theology of the Dwelling Place of God.* Downers Grove, IL: InterVarsity Press, 2004.

Beckwith, Roger. *The Old Testament Canon of the New Testament Church.* Grand Rapids, MI: Eerdmans, 1985.

Ben-Daniel, John, and Gloria Ben-Daniel. *The Apocalypse in the Light of the Temple: A New Approach to the Book of Revelation.* Jerusalem: Beit Yochanan, 2003.

Benin, Stephen D. *The Footprints of God: Divine Accommodation in Jewish and Christian Thought.* Albany, NY: SUNY Press, 1993.

Berger, David. *Thomas Aquinas & the Liturgy.* Naples, FL: Sapientia Press, 2004.

Biderman, Shlomo. *Scripture & Knowledge: An Essay on Religious Epistemology.* Leiden: Brill, 1995.

Bonaventure. *De Reductione Artium ad Theologiam.* Saint Bonaventure, NY: The Franciscan Institute, 1955.

Bonneau, Normand, O.M.I. *Preparing the Table of the Word.* Collegeville, MN: Liturgical Press, 1997.

Bonneau, Normand, O.M.I. *The Sunday Lectionary: Ritual Word, Paschal Shape.* Collegeville, MN: Liturgical Press, 1998.

Bouley, Allan, O.S.B. *From Freedom to Formula: The Evolution of the Eucharistic Prayer from Oral Improvisation to Written Texts.* Washington, DC: Catholic University of America Press, 1981.

Bouyer, Louis. *The Christian Mystery: From Pagan Myth to Christian Mysticism.* Edinburgh: T. & T. Clark, 1990.

———. *Eucharist: Theology and Spirituality of the Eucharistic Prayer.* Notre Dame, IN: University of Notre Dame, 1968.

———. *Liturgical Piety.* Notre Dame, IN: University of Notre Dame, 1955.

———. *Rite and Man.* London: Burns and Oates, 1963.

———. *The Spirit and Forms of Protestantism.* Westminster, MD: Newman Press, 1961.

———. *The Spirituality of the New Testament and the Fathers.* New York: Seabury, 1960.

———. *The Word, Church and Sacraments in Protestantism and Catholicism.* San Francisco: Ignatius Press, 2004.

Bowler, C. P., S.M., M.A. *Living the Truth.* Authorized reprint. Melbourne: 2004.

Boxall, Ian. *Revelation: Vision and Insight.* London: SPCK, 2002.

Boyer, Mark G. *Mystagogy: Liturgical Paschal Spirituality for Lent and Easter.* New York: Alba House, 1990.

Bradshaw, Paul F. *The Search for the Origins of Christian Worship: Sources and Methods for the Study of Early Liturgy.* Second edition. New York: Oxford University Press, 2002.

Breck, John. *Scripture in Tradition: The Bible and Its Interpretation in the Orthodox Church.* Crestwood, NY: St. Vladimir's Seminary Press, 2001.

Breck, John. *The Power of the Word in the Worshiping Church*. Crestwood, NY: St. Vladimir's Seminary Press, 1986.

Brennenman, James E. *Canons in Conflict: Negotiating Texts in True and False Prophecy*. New York: Oxford University Press, 1997.

Brichto, H. C. *The Problem of "Curse" in the Hebrew Bible*. Philadelphia: Society of Biblical Literature, 1963.

Briggs, Richard S. *Words in Action: Speech Act Theory and Biblical Interpretation*. Edinburgh: T. & T. Clark, 2001.

Briggs, Robert A. *Jewish Temple Imagery in the Book of Revelation*. New York: Peter Lang Publishing, 1999.

Brightman, F. E. *Liturgies Eastern and Western*. Oxford: Clarendon Press, 1896.

Brown, Raymond E. *An Introduction to the Gospel of John*. Edited by Francis J. Moloney. New York: Doubleday, 2003.

———. *New Testament Essays*. New York: Doubleday, 1968.

———. *The Semitic Background of the Term "Mystery in the New Testament."* Philadelphia: Fortress Press, 1968.

Bruce, F. F. *The Canon of Scripture*. Downers Grove, IL: InterVarsity Press, 1988.

Brueggemann, Walter. *The Book That Breathes New Life: Scriptural Authority and Biblical Theology*. Minneapolis, MN: Fortress Press, 2005.

Buchanan, G. W. *Typology and the Gospel*. New York: University Press of America, 1984.

Burgard, Charles. *Scripture in the Liturgy*. Westminster, MD: Newman Press, 1960.

Burgess, John P. *Why Scripture Matters: Reading the Bible in a Time of Church Conflict*. Louisville, KY: Westminster John Knox Press, 1998.

Burke, John, O.P., and Thomas P. Doyle, O.P. *The Homilist's Guide to Scripture, Theology, and Canon Law*. New York: Pueblo Publishing Company, 1986.

Burkert, Walter. *Creation of the Sacred*. Cambridge, MA: Harvard University Press, 1996.

Burtchaell, James Tunstead. *From Synagogue to Church: Public Services and Offices in the Earliest Christian Communities.* Cambridge: Cambridge University Press, 1992.

Burton-Christie, Douglas. *The Word in the Desert: Scripture and the Quest for Holiness in Early Christian Monasticism.* New York: Oxford University Press, 1993.

Cabasilas, Nicholas. *A Commentary on the Divine Liturgy.* London: SPCK, 1983.

Caldecott, Stratford, ed. *Beyond the Prosaic: Renewing the Liturgical Movement.* Edinburgh: T. & T. Clark, 1998.

Cantalamessa, Raniero, O.F.M. Cap. *Easter in the Early Church.* Collegeville, MN: Liturgical Press, 1993.

———. *The Mystery of God's Word.* Collegeville, MN: Liturgical Press, 1994.

Carlebach, Elisheva, John M. Efron, and David N. Myers, eds. *Jewish History and Jewish Memory: Essays in Honor of Yosef Hayim Yerushalmi.* Hanover, NH: Brandeis University Press, 1998.

Carr, David. *Time, Narrative, and History.* Indianapolis, IN: Indiana University Press, 1991.

Cartledge, T. *Vows in the Hebrew Bible and the Ancient Near East.* Sheffield: JSOT, 1992.

Casel, Odo, O.S.B. *The Mystery of Christian Worship.* Westminster, MD: Newman Press, 1962.

Cavalletti, Sofia. "Memorial and Typology in Jewish and Christian Liturgy," *Letter & Spirit* (2005): 70–86.

———. *History's Golden Thread: The History of Salvation.* Oak Park, IL: Catechesis of the Good Shepherd Publications, 1999.

———. *Living Liturgy: Elementary Reflections.* Oak Park, IL: Catechesis of the Good Shepherd Publications, 1998.

Cavanaugh, William T. *Theopolitical Imagination: Discovering the Liturgy as a Political Act in an Age of Global Consumerism.* Edinburgh: T. & T. Clark, 2002.

Cavanaugh, William T. *Torture and Eucharist.* Oxford: Blackwell Publishers, 1998.

Charlesworth, James H., ed. *Old Testament Pseudepigrapha.* New York: Doubleday, 1983.

Chauvet, Louis-Marie. *Symbol and Sacrament: A Sacramental Reinterpretation of Christian Existence.* Collegeville, MN: Liturgical Press, 1995.

Chenderlin, Fritz. *"Do This As My Memorial."* Rome: Biblical Institute Press, 1982.

Chilton, Bruce. *Redeeming Time: The Wisdom of Ancient Jewish and Christian Festal Calendars.* Peabody, MA: Hendrickson, 2002.

Clément, Olivier. *The Roots of Christian Mysticism.* London: New City Press, 1995.

Collins, John J. *The Scepter and the Star: The Messiahs of the Dead Sea Scrolls and Other Ancient Literature.* New York: Doubleday, 1995.

Congar, Yves M.-J., O.P. *The Meaning of Tradition.* San Francisco: Ignatius Press, 2004.

———. *Tradition and Traditions.* New York: MacMillan, 1966.

Connolly, James M. *Human History and the Word of God: The Christian Meaning of History in Contemporary Thought.* New York: MacMillan, 1965.

Cook, J. I., ed. *Grace Upon Grace.* Grand Rapids, MI: Eerdmans, 1975.

Cooke, Bernard J., S.J. *Christian Sacraments and Christian Personality.* New York: Holt, Rinehart and Winston, 1965.

Corbin, Henry. *Temple and Contemplation.* London: Islamic Publications Limited, 1968.

Corbon, Jean. *The Wellspring of Worship.* New York: Paulist Press, 1988.

Corriveau, Raymond, C.SS.R. *The Liturgy of Life: A Study of the Ethical Thought of St. Paul in His Letter to the Early Christian Communities.* Brussels: Desclée de Brouwer, 1970.

Costello, Charles Joseph, S.T.L. *St. Augustine's Doctrine of the Inspiration and Canonicity of Scripture.* Washington, DC: Catholic University of America Press, 1930.

Crawford, T. G. *Blessing and Curse in Syro-Palestinian Inscriptions.* New York: Peter Lang, 1992.

Cross, F. M. *From Epic to Canon: History and Literature in Ancient Israel.* Baltimore: Johns Hopkins University Press, 1998.

Crowe, Frederick E., S.J. *Theology of the Christian Word: A Study in History.* New York: Paulist Press, 1978.

Cullmann, Oscar. *Early Christian Worship.* London: SCM Press, 1956.

Cullmann, Oscar, and F. J. Leenhardt. *Essays on the Lord's Supper.* London: Lutterworth Press, 1958.

Cuming, Geoffrey J., ed. *The Liturgy of St. Mark.* Rome: Pontifical Oriental Institute, 1990.

Cyril of Jerusalem. *On the Christian Sacraments.* Edited by F. L. Cross. Crestwood, NY: St. Vladimir's Seminary Press, 1977.

Daley, Brian E. *The Hope of the Early Church: A Handbook of Patristic Eschatology.* Peabody, MA: Hendrickson, 2003.

Dalmais, I. H., O.P. *Introduction to the Liturgy.* Baltimore: Helicon Press, 1961.

Daly, Robert J., S.J. *Christian Sacrifice: The Judaeo-Christian Background Before Origen.* Washington, DC: Catholic University of America Press, 1978.

Danielou, Jean, S.J. *From Shadows to Reality: Studies in the Typology of the Fathers.* London: Burns and Oates, 1960.

———. *The Angels and Their Mission: According to the Fathers of the Church.* Notre Dame, IN: Ave Maria Press, 1987.

———. *The Bible and the Liturgy.* Notre Dame, IN: Notre Dame University Press, 1956.

———. *The Lord of History.* New York: Meridian, 1968.

———. *The Presence of God.* Baltimore: Helicon Press, 1959.

Davidson, R. M. *Typology in Scripture: A Study of Hermeneutical* Tupos *Structures.* Berrien Springs, MI: Andrews University Press, 1981.

Davis, Charles. *Liturgy and Doctrine.* London: Sheed and Ward, 1960.

Dawson, J. D. *Christian Figural Reading and the Fashioning of Identity.* Berkeley: University of California Press, 2002.

Deiss, Lucien, C.S.Sp. *Celebration of the Word.* Collegeville, MN: Liturgical Press, 1993.

———. *God's Word and God's People.* Collegeville, MN: Liturgical Press, 1976.

DeLeers, Stephen Vincent. *The Vision and Practice of Sunday Preaching.* Collegeville, MN: The Liturgical Press, 2004.

de Lubac, Henri, S.J. *Medieval Exegesis.* 2 vols. Grand Rapids, MI: Eerdmans, 1998, 2000.

———. *Scripture in the Tradition.* New York: The Crossroad Publisher Company, 2000.

de Margerie, Bertrand, S.J. *The Greek Fathers.* Petersham, MA: St. Bede's, 1993.

de Vaux, Roland, O.P. *Ancient Israel: Its Life and Institutions.* New York: McGraw-Hill, 1965.

Dillenschneider, Clement, C.Ss.R. *Christ the One Priest and We His Priests.* 2 vols. St. Louis, MO: B. Herder Book Co., 1964.

———. *The Holy Spirit and the Priest.* St. Louis, MO: B. Herder Book Co., 1965.

———. *The Dynamic Power of Our Sacraments.* St. Louis, MO: B. Herder Book Co., 1966.

Dix, Dom Gregory. *The Shape of the Liturgy.* New York: Seabury, 1982.

Documents on the Liturgy 1963–1979: Conciliar, Papal, and Curial Texts. Collegeville, MN: Liturgical Press, 1982.

Doran, Robert M. *Theology and the Dialectics of History.* Toronto: University of Toronto Press, 1990.

Dozeman, Thomas B. "The Holiness of God in Contemporary Jewish and Christian Biblical Theology." In *God's Word for Our World.* 2 vols. Edited by Harold J. Ellens. London: T. & T. Clark, 2004.

Driscoll, Jeremy. *Theology at the Eucharistic Table.* Rome: Studia Anselmiana, 2003.

Driscoll, Jeremy. *What Happens at Mass.* Chicago, IL: Liturgy Training Publications, 2005.

Duchesne, Louis. *Christian Worship.* London: SPCK, 1923.

Durrwell, F. X. *The Eucharist: Presence of Christ.* Denville, NJ: Dimension Books, 1974.

Durrwell, F. X. *FX Durrwell C.Ss.R.* London: Sheed and Ward, 1972.

Eden, Kathy. *Hermeneutics and the Rhetorical Tradition: Chapters in the Ancient Legacy and Its Humanist Reception.* New Haven, CT: Yale University Press, 1997.

Elior, Rachel. *The Three Temples: On the Emergence of Jewish Mysticism.* Portland, OR: The Littman Library of Jewish Civilization, 2004.

Elliot, Charles. *Memory and Salvation.* London: Darton, Longman and Todd, 1995.

Ellis, E. E. *The Making of the New Testament Documents.* Leiden: Brill, 1999.

Ernest, James D. *The Bible in Athanasius of Alexandria.* Leiden: Brill, 2004.

Esposito, Rosario F., ed. *Carissimi in San Paolo: Lettere, Articoli, Opuscoli, Scritti Inediti di Don Giaccomo Alberione dal 1933 al 1969.* Rome: Edizioni Paoline, 1971.

Eusebius. *Ecclesiastical History.* Grand Rapids, MI: Baker Book House, 1974.

Evans, Donald D. *The Logic of Self-Involvement.* New York: Herder and Herder, 1969.

Evans, Helen C. *The Arts of Byzantium.* New York: Metropolitan Museum of Art, 2001.

Ezra, Daniel Stokl Ben. *The Impact of Yom Kippur on Early Christianity: The Day of Atonement from Second Temple Judaism to the Fifth Century.* Tubingen: Mohr Siebeck, 2003.

Fagerberg, David W. *Theologia Prima: What Is Liturgical Theology?* Chicago: Hillenbrand Books, 2004.

Farmer, William R., and Denis M. Farkasfalvy, O.Cist. *The Formation of the New Testament Canon: An Ecumenical Approach.* New York: Paulist Press, 1983.

Farrer, A. *A Rebirth of Images: The Making of St. John's Apocalypse.* London: Dacre Press, 1948.

Farrow, Douglas. *Ascension and Ecclesia.* Grand Rapids, MI: Eerdmans, 1999.

Feeley-Harnick, Gillian. *The Lord's Table: The Meaning of Food in Early Judaism and Christianity.* Washington, DC: Smithsonian Institution, 1982.

Field, John Edward. *The Apostolic Liturgy and the Epistle to the Hebrews.* London: Rivingtons, 1882.

Finkelman, Rabbi Shimon. *Shabbos: The Sabbath—Its Essence and Significance.* Brooklyn, NY: Mesorah Publications, 1991.

Fisch, Thomas, ed. *Liturgy and Tradition: Theological Reflections of Alexander Schmemann.* Crestwood, NY: St. Vladimir's Seminary Press, 1990.

Fishbane, Michael. *Text and Texture: Close Readings of Selected Biblical Texts.* New York: Schocken Books, 1979.

Fisher, Eugene J., ed. *The Jewish Roots of Christian Liturgy.* New York: Paulist Press, 1990.

Fletcher-Louis, Crispin H. T. *All the Glory of Adam: Liturgical Anthropology in the Dead Sea Scrolls.* Leiden: Brill, 2002.

Fowl, Stephen E. *Engaging Scripture.* Malden, MA: Blackwell Publishers, 1998.

Frend, W. H. C. *The Early Church.* Minneapolis, MN: Fortress Press, 1982.

Frend, W. H. C. *The Rise of Christianity.* Philadelphia: Fortress Press, 1984.

Froehlich, Karlfried. *Biblical Interpretation in the Early Church.* Philadelphia: Fortress Press, 1984.

Frye, Northrop. *The Great Code: The Bible and Literature.* New York: Harvest/HBJ, 1982.

Garraghan, Gilbert J., S.J. *A Guide to Historical Method.* New York: Fordham University Press, 1946.

Gavin, F. *The Jewish Antecedents of the Christian Sacraments.* New York: Ktav Publishing House, 1969.

Gese, Hartmut. *Essays on Biblical Theology.* Minneapolis, MN: Augsburg Publishing House, 1981.

Gilders, William K. *Blood Ritual in the Hebrew Bible: Meaning and Power.* Baltimore: Johns Hopkins University Press, 2004.

Glatzer, Nahum N., ed. *The Passover Haggadah.* New York: Schocken, 1989.

Goldingay, John. *Models for Scripture.* Grand Rapids, MI: Eerdmans, 1994.

———. *Models for Interpretation of Scripture.* Grand Rapids, MI: Eerdmans, 1995.

Goppelt, L. *Typos: The Typological Interpretation of the Old Testament in the New.* Grand Rapids, MI: Eerdmans, 1982.

Goulder, M. D. *The Evangelists' Calendar: A Lectionary Explanation of the Development of Scripture.* London: SPCK, 1978.

———. *Type and History in Acts.* London: SPCK, 1964.

Graham, P., ed. *The Chronicler as Theologian: Essays in Honor of Ralph W. Klein.* London: T. & T. Clark, 2003.

Graham, William A. *Beyond the Written Word: Oral Aspects of Scripture in the History of Religion.* Cambridge: Cambridge University Press, 1987.

Grasso, Domenico, S.J. *Proclaiming God's Message: A Study in the Theology of Preaching.* Notre Dame, IN: University of Notre Dame Press, 1965.

Green, Joel B., and Michael Pasquarello III, eds. *Narrative Reading, Narrative Preaching: New Testament Interpretation and Proclamation.* Grand Rapids, MI: Baker Academic, 2003.

Greenberg, Irving. *For the Sake of Heaven and Earth: The New Encounter Between Judaism and Christianity.* Philadelphia: The Jewish Publication Society, 2004.

Griffiths, J. G. *The Divine Verdict: A Study of Divine Judgement in the Ancient Religions.* Leiden: Brill, 1991.

Gruenwald, Ithamar. *Rituals and Ritual Theory in Ancient Israel.* Leiden: Brill, 2003.

Guardini, Romano. *Meditations Before Mass.* Manchester, NH: Sophia Institute Press, 1993.

Guilday, Peter, ed. *The Catholic Philosophy of History.* Freeport, NY: Books for Libraries Press, Inc., 1967.

Haffner, Paul. *The Sacramental Mystery.* England: Gracewing, 1999.

Hahn, Scott. "A Broken Covenant and the Curse-of-Death: A Study of Hebrews 9:15–22." *Catholic Biblical Quarterly* 66, no. 3 (July 2004): 416–36.

―――. "Canon, Cult, and Covenant: Towards a Liturgical Hermeneutic," in *Canon Criticism and Theological Interpretation,* eds. Craig Bartholomew et al. Grand Rapids, MI: Forthcoming 2006.

―――. "Covenant, Cult, and the Curse-of-Death: *Diatheke* in Hebrews 9:15–22," in *Hebrews: Contemporary Methods—New Insights,* ed. Gabriella Gelardini. Leiden: Brill, 2005.

―――. "Covenant in the Old and New Testaments: Some Current Research (1994–2004)." *Currents in Biblical Research* 3, no. 2 (2005): 263–292.

―――. "Covenant Oath and the Aqedah: *Diatheke* in Galatians 3:15–18." *Catholic Biblical Quarterly* 67, no. 1 (January 2005): 79–100.

―――. *A Father Who Keeps His Promises: God's Covenant Love in Scripture.* Ann Arbor, MI: Servant, 1998.

————. *First Comes Love: Finding Your Family in the Church and the Trinity.* New York: Doubleday, 2002.

————. *Hail, Holy Queen: The Mother of God in the Word of God.* New York: Doubleday, 2001.

————. "Kingdom and Church in Luke–Acts: From Davidic Christology to Kingdom Ecclesiology," in *Reading Luke,* eds. Craig Bartholomew et al. Grand Rapids, MI: Zondervan 2005, pp. 294–326.

————. *Lord, Have Mercy: The Healing Power of Confession.* New York, Doubleday, 2003.

————. "Passionately Loving the Word: The Use of Scripture in the Writings of Blessed Josemaria." *Romana* 35 (July–December 2002): 382–90.

————. *Scripture Matters: Essays on Reading the Bible from the Heart of the Church.* Steubenville, OH: Emmaus Road, 2003.

————. *Swear to God: The Promise and Power of the Sacraments.* New York: Doubleday, 2004.

————. *The Lamb's Supper: The Mass as Heaven on Earth.* New York: Doubleday, 1999.

————. *Understanding the Scriptures: A Complete Course on Bible Study.* Chicago: Midwest Theological Forum, 2005.

Hahn, Scott, and Mike Aquilina. *Living the Mysteries: A Guide for Unfinished Christians.* Huntington, IN: Our Sunday Visitor, 2003.

Hahn, Scott, and John Sietze Bergsma. "Noah's Nakedness and the Curse on Canaan (Genesis 9:20–27)." *Journal of Biblical Literature* 124, no. 1 (Spring 2005): 25–40.

Hahn, Scott, and John Sietze Bergsma. "What Laws Were 'Not Good'? A Canonical Approach to the Theological Problem of Ezekiel 20:25–26." *Journal of Biblical Literature* 123, no. 2 (Summer 2004): 201–18.

Hagen, Kenneth, ed. *The Quadrilog: Tradition and the Future of Ecumenism: Essays in Honor of George H. Tavard.* Collegeville, MN: Liturgical Press, 1994.

Halbertal, Moshe. *People of the Book: Canon, Meaning, and Authority.* Cambridge, MA: Harvard University Press, 1997.

Hall, Christopher A. *Reading Scripture with the Church Fathers.* Downers Grove, IL: InterVarsity Press, 1998.

Hall, Jerome M. *We Have the Mind of Christ: The Holy Spirit and Liturgical Memory in the Thought of Edward J. Kilmartin.* Collegeville, MN: Liturgical Press, 2001.

Hanson, R. P. C. *Origen's Doctrine of Tradition.* London: SPCK, 1954.

Harmless, William. *Augustine and the Catechumenate.* Collegeville, MN: Liturgical Press, 1995.

Harris, R. Laird. *Inspiration and Canonicity of the Bible.* Grand Rapids, MI: Zondervan, 1969.

Harrison, Peter. *The Bible, Protestantism, and the Rise of Natural Science.* Cambridge: Cambridge University Press, 1998.

Hauerwas, Stanley. *Unleashing the Scripture: Freeing the Bible from Captivity to America.* Nashville, TN: Abingdon, 1993.

Hauser, Daniel C. *Church, Worship and History: Catholic Systematic Theology.* San Francisco: Catholic Scholars Press, 1997.

Hay, David M., ed. *Both Literal and Allegorical: Studies in Philo Alexandria's* Questions and Answers on Genesis and Exodus. Atlanta, GA: Scholars Press, 1991.

Hebert, A. G. *The Throne of David: A Study of the Fulfillment of the Old Testament in Jesus Christ and His Church.* London: Faber & Faber, 1942.

Helmer, Christine, and Christof Landmesser, eds. *One Scripture or Many? Canon from Biblical, Theological and Philosophical Perspectives.* New York: Oxford University Press, 2004.

Herron, T. J. *The Dating of the First Epistle of Clement to the Corinthians.* Rome: Pontifical Gregorian University, 1987.

Hervieu-Léger, Danièle. *Religion as a Chain of Memory.* New Brunswick, NJ: Rutgers University Press, 2000.

Heschel, Abraham Joshua. *The Sabbath: Its Meaning for Modern Man.* New York: Farrar, Straus and Young, 1951.

Heyduck, Richard. *The Recovery of Doctrine in the Contemporary Church: An Essay in Philosophical Ecclesiology.* Waco, TX: Baylor University Press, 2002.

Hill, Andrew E. *Enter His Courts with Praise!: Old Testament Worship for the New Testament Church.* Nashville, TN: Star Song Publishing Group, 1993.

Hippolytus. *On the Apostolic Tradition.* Edited by Alistair Stewart-Sykes. Crestwood, NY: St. Vladimir's Seminary Press, 2001.

Hippolytus. *The Apostolic Tradition.* London: SPCK, 1937.

Hippolytus. *The Apostolic Tradition of Hippolytus.* London: Cambridge University, 1934.

Holmes, Stephen R. *Listening to the Past: The Places of Tradition in Theology.* Grand Rapids, MI: Baker Academic, 2002.

Homan, Michael M. *To Your Tents, O Israel! The Terminology, Function, Form, and Symbolism of Tents in the Hebrew Bible and Ancient Near East.* Leiden: Brill, 2002.

Houtman, A., M. Poorthuis, and J. Schwartz. *Sanctity of Time and Space in Tradition and Modernity.* Leiden: Brill, 1998.

Hugenberger, Gordon P. *Marriage as a Covenant: Biblical Law and Ethics as Developed from Malachi.* Grand Rapids, MI: Baker Books, 1998.

Hugh of St. Victor. *The Didascalicon of Hugh of St. Victor.* New York: Columbia University Press, 1961.

Hunter, David G., ed. *Preaching in the Patristic Age: Studies in Honor of Walter J. Burghardt, S.J.* New York: Paulist Press, 1989.

Hutton, Patrick H. *History as an Art of Memory.* Hanover, NH: University Press of New England, 1993.

Irenaeus of Lyons. *St. Irenaeus of Lyons: Against the Heresies.* New York: Paulist Press, 1992.

Isaacs, Marie E. *Sacred Space: An Approach to the Theology of the Epistle to the Hebrews.* Sheffield: Sheffield Academic, 1992.

Jacobs, Alan. *A Theology of Reading: The Hermeneutics of Love.* Boulder, CO: Westview Press, 2001.

Janowiak, Paul, S.J. *The Holy Preaching: The Sacramentality of the Word in the Liturgical Assembly.* Collegeville, MN: Liturgical Press, 2000.

Jeffrey, David Lyle. *People of the Book: Christian Identity and Literary Culture.* Grand Rapids, MI: Eerdmans, 1996.

Jeremias, Joachim. *The Eucharistic Words of Jesus.* London: SCM, 1966.

John Chrysostom. *St. John Chrysostom: Baptismal Instructions.* Westminster, MD: Newman Press, 1963.

————. *On the Priesthood*. Crestwood, NY: St. Vladimir's Seminary Press, 2002.

Johnson, Maxwell E. *The Prayers of Sarapion of Thmuis: A Literary, Liturgical, and Theological Analysis*. Rome: Pontifical Oriental Institute, 1995.

Jones, Cheslyn et al., eds. *The Study of Liturgy*. London: SPCK, 1992.

Josephus. *Works of Josephus: Complete and Unabridged*. Peabody, MA: Hendrickson, 1987.

Jungmann, Josef, S.J. *Announcing the Word of God*. New York: Herder and Herder, 1967.

Jungmann, Josef, S.J. *The Early Liturgy*. Notre Dame, IN: Notre Dame University Press, 1959.

————. *The Eucharistic Prayer*. Notre Dame, IN: Fides, 1964.

————. *Handing on the Faith*. New York: Herder and Herder, 1962.

————. *The Mass of the Roman Rite: Its Origins and Development*. 2 vols. Allen, TX: Christian Classics, 1986.

Kakkanatt, Antony. *Christological Catechesis of the Liturgy: A Study on the Great Feasts of Our Lord in the Malankara Church*. Rome: Mar Thoma Yogam, 1996.

Karavites, P. *Promise-Giving and Treaty-Making: Homer and the Near East*. Leiden: Brill, 1992.

Katz, Steven T., ed. *Mysticism and Sacred Scripture*. Oxford: Oxford University Press, 2000.

Kavanagh, Aidan. *On Liturgical Theology*. New York: Pueblo Publishing Company, 1984.

Keefe, Donald J. *Covenantal Theology: The Eucharistic Order of History*. 2 vols. New York: University Press of America, 1991.

Kennard, Douglas Welker, ed. *The Relationship Between Epistemology, Hermeneutics, Biblical Theology and Contextualization*. Lewiston, NY: Edwin Mellen Press, 1999.

Kelsey, David H. *The Uses of Scripture in Recent Theology*. Philadelphia: Fortress Press, 1975.

Kereszty, Roch. "The Eucharist in the Letter to the Hebrews." *Communio* 26 (1999): 154–67.

Kilmartin, Edward J., S.J. *Christian Liturgy: Theology and Practice.* Kansas City, MO: Sheed & Ward, 1988.

Kitchen, Robert A., and Martien F. G. Parmentier, trans. *The Book of Steps: The Syriac Liber Graduum.* Kalamazoo, MI: Cistercian Publications, 2004.

Kleinig, John W. *The Lord's Song: The Basis, Function and Significance of Choral Music in Chronicles.* Sheffield: Sheffield Academic Press, 1993.

Kline, Meredith G. *By Oath Consigned: A Reinterpretation of the Covenant Signs of Circumcision and Baptism.* Grand Rapids, MI: Eerdmans, 1968.

———. *The Structure of Biblical Authority.* Revised edition. Grand Rapids, MI: Eerdmans, 1972.

Kodell, Jerome, O.S.B. *The Eucharist in the New Testament.* Collegeville, MN: Liturgical Press, 1991.

Koenig, John. *The Feast of the World's Redemption: Eucharistic Origins and Christian Mission.* Harrisburg, PA: Trinity Press International, 2000.

———. *God's Word at Mass.* New York: Hawthorn, 1967.

Koenker, Ernest Benjamin. *The Liturgical Renaissance in the Roman Catholic Church.* Chicago: The University of Chicago Press, 1954.

Kollamparambil, Antony George. *From Symbol to Truth: A Syriac Understanding of the Paschal Mystery.* Rome: Centro Liturgico Vincenziano, 2000.

———. *The Life-Giving Paschal Lamb.* Kerala, India: HIRS Publications, 1997.

Kottackal, Joseph. *The Salvific Folly of God: A Biblical-Theological Study of the Paradox of God's Folly and the World's Wisdom.* Kerala, India: Oriental Institute for Religious Studies India, 1994.

Kraus, Hans-Joachim. *Worship in Israel.* Richmond, VA: John Knox Press, 1966.

Kucharek, Casimir. *The Sacramental Mysteries: A Byzantine Approach.* Combermere, Ontario: Alleluia Press, 1976.

Kuntzmann, R. *Typologie Biblique.* Paris: Cerf, 2002.

Kunzler, Michael. *The Church's Liturgy.* New York: The Continuum International Publishing Group, 2001.

Laato, Antti, and Johannes C. de Moor. *Theodicy in the World of the Bible.* Leiden: Brill, 2003.

Lampe, G. W. H., and K. J. Woollcombe. *Essays on Typology.* London: SCM Press, 1957.

Langan, Thomas. *Being and Truth.* Columbia, MO: University of Missouri Press, 1996.

————. *The Catholic Tradition.* Columbia, MO: University of Missouri Press, 1998.

————. *Tradition and Authenticity in the Search for Ecumenic Wisdom.* Columbia, MO: University of Missouri Press, 1992.

LaPorte, Jean. *Eucharistia in Philo.* New York: Edwin Mellen, 1983.

————. "Philonic Models of Eucharistia in the Eucharist of Origen." *Laval théologique et philosophique* 42, no. 1 (February 1986): 71–91.

LaPorte, Jean, and Finian Taylor. *Understanding Our Biblical and Early Christian Tradition: An Introductory Textbook in Theology.* Ceredigion, United Kingdom: The Edwin Mellen Press, 1991.

Lathrop, Gordon W. *Holy Ground: A Liturgical Cosmology.* Minneapolis, MN: Fortress Press, 2003.

————. *Holy People: A Liturgical Ecclesiology.* Minneapolis, MN: Fortress Press, 1999.

————. *Holy Things: A Liturgical Theology.* Minneapolis, MN: Fortress Press, 1993.

LaVerdiere, Eugene. *The Eucharist in the New Testament and the Early Church.* Collegeville, MN: Liturgical Press, 1996.

————. "The Loaves and Fish, A Eucharistic Banquet." *The Bible Today,* vol. 40, no. 4 229–35.

Leclercq, Jean, O.S.B. *The Love of Learning and the Desire for God: A Study of Monastic Culture.* New York: Fordham University Press, 1961.

Ledegang, F. *Mysterium Ecclesiae: Images of the Church and Its Members in Origen.* Leuven: Leuven University Press, 2001.

Le Goff, Jacques. *History and Memory.* New York: Columbia University Press, 1992.

Leithart, Peter J. *From Silence to Song: The Davidic Liturgical Revolution.* Moscow, ID: Canon Press, 2003.

Leithart, Peter J. *The Kingdom and the Power: Rediscovering the Centrality of the Church.* Phillipsburg, NJ: P&R Publishing, 1993.

————. *Priesthood of the Plebs: A Theology of Baptism.* Eugene, OR: Wipf and Stock Publishers, 2003.

Levenson, Jon D. *Sinai & Zion: An Entry into the Jewish Bible.* New York: Winston Press, 1985.

Levine, Baruch. *In the Presence of the Lord: A Study of Cult and Some Cultic Terms in Ancient Israel.* Leiden: Brill, 1974.

———. *Leviticus.* The JPS Torah Commentary. Philadelphia: Jewish Publication Society, 1989.

Lienhard, Joseph T. *The Bible, the Church, and Authority: The Canon of the Christian Bible in History and Theology.* Collegeville, MN: Liturgical Press, 1995.

Lightfoot, J. B., and J. R. Harmer, eds. *The Apostolic Fathers.* London: Macmillan, 1891.

Little, Edmund. *Echoes of the Old Testament in the Wine of Cana in Galilee (John 2:1–11) and the Multiplication of the Loaves and Fish (John 6:1–15): Towards an Appreciation.* Paris: J. Gabalda, 1998.

Loisy, Alfred. *The Gospel and the Church.* Philadelphia: Fortress Press, 1976.

Loretz, Oswald. *The Truth of the Bible.* New York: Herder and Herder, 1968.

Louth, Andrew. *Denys the Areopagite.* New York: Continuum, 2001.

———. *Discerning the Mystery: An Essay on the Nature of Theology.* Oxford: Clarendon Press, 1983.

———. *Maximus the Confessor.* New York: Routledge, 1996.

Luttikhuizen, Gerard P. *Paradise Interpreted: Representations of Biblical Paradise in Judaism and Christianity.* Leiden: Brill, 1999.

Luxon, Thomas H. *Literal Figures: Puritan Allegory and the Reformation Crisis in Representation.* Chicago: University of Chicago Press, 1995.

MacKenzie, Iain M. *Irenaeus's Demonstration of the Apostolic Preaching: A Theological Commentary and Translation.* Burlington, VT: Ashgate Publishing Company, 2002.

Mackey, J. P. *The Modern Theology of Tradition.* London: Darton, Longman & Todd, 1962.

Madsen, Truman G., ed. *The Temple in Antiquity: Ancient Records and Modern Perspectives.* Provo, UT: Brigham Young University, 1984.

Magnetti, D. L. *The Oath in the Old Testament in the Light of Related Terms and in the Legal and Covenantal Context of the Ancient Near East.* Ph.D. dissertation. Johns Hopkins University, 1969.

Magsam, Charles M. *The Inner Life of Worship.* St. Meinrad, IN: Grail Publications, 1958.

Maly, Eugene. "Israel—God's Liturgical People." In *Liturgy for the People: Essays in Honor of Gerald Ellard, S.J.* Edited by William J. Leonard, S.J. Milwaukee, WI: Bruce, 1963.

Maniyattu, P. *Heaven on Earth: The Theology of Liturgical Space-Time in the East Syrian Curbana.* Rome: Mar Thoma Yogam, 1995.

Mannion, M. Francis. *Masterworks of God: Essays in Liturgical Theory and Practice.* Mundelein, IL: Hillenbrand Books, 2004.

———. "Rejoice, Heavenly Powers: The Renewal of Liturgical Doxology." *Pro Ecclesia* 12, no. 1 2003: 37–60.

Marrou, Henri. *The Meaning of History.* Baltimore: Helicon Press Ltd., 1966.

Martimort, A. G., ed. *The Church at Prayer.* Collegeville, MN: Liturgical Press, 1992.

Martimort, A. G. *The Signs of the New Covenant.* Collegeville, MN: Liturgical Press, 1963.

Mathewson, David. *A New Heaven and a New Earth: The Meaning and Function of the Old Testament in Revelation 21:1–22:5.* Sheffield: Sheffield Academic Press, 2003.

Maximus the Confessor. *Maximus Confessor: Selected Writings.* New York: Paulist Press, 1985.

———. *The Church, the Liturgy, and the Soul of Man.* Still River, MA: St. Bede's Publications, 1982.

Mazza, Enrico. *Mystagogy: A Theology of Liturgy in the Patristic Age.* New York: Pueblo, 1989.

Mazza, Enrico. *The Celebration of the Eucharist: The Origin of the Rite and the Development of Its Interpretation.* Collegeville, MN: Pueblo, 1999.

———. *The Origins of the Eucharistic Prayer.* Collegeville, MN: Pueblo, 1995.

McAuliffe, Jane Dammen, Barry D. Walfish, and Joseph W. Goering. *With Reverence for the Word: Medieval Scriptural Exegesis in Judaism, Christianity, and Islam.* Oxford: Oxford University Press, 2003.

McDonald, Lee M. *The Formation of the Christian Biblical Canon: Revised & Expanded Edition.* Peabody, MA: Hendrickson, 1995.

McDonald, Lee Martin, and James A. Sanders, eds. *The Canon Debate.* Peabody, MA: Hendrickson, 2002.

McDonough, William K. *The Divine Family: The Trinity and Our Life in God.* New York: Macmillan, 1963.

McGinn, Bernard, and John Meyendorff, eds. *Christian Spirituality: Origins to the Twelfth Century.* New York: Crossroad, 1989.

McGoldrick, Patrick. "Liturgy: The Context of Patristic Exegesis," in *Scriptural Interpretation in the Fathers: Letter and Spirit.* Edited by Vincent Twomey. Dublin: Four Courts Press, 1995.

McGovern, Thomas J. *Priestly Identity: A Study in the Theology of Priesthood.* Dublin: Four Courts Press, 2002.

McKenna, John H. *Eucharist and Holy Spirit: The Eucharistic Epiclesis in 20th Century Theology.* England: Mayhew-McCrimmon, 1975.

McLay, R. Timothy. *The Use of the Septuagint in New Testament Research.* Grand Rapids, MI: Eerdmans, 2003.

Meade, David G. *Pseudonymity and Canon: An Investigation into the Relationship of Authorship and Authority in Jewish and Earliest Christian Tradition.* Grand Rapids, MI: Eerdmans, 1986.

Melito of Sardis. *On Pascha and Fragments.* Oxford: Clarendon, 1979.

Mettinger, T. N. D. *In Search of God: The Meaning and Message of the Everlasting Names.* Philadelphia: Fortress Press, 1988.

Meurer, Siegfried, ed. *The Apocrypha in Ecumenical Perspective.* New York: United Bible Societies, 1991.

Meyer, Marvin W., ed. *The Ancient Mysteries: A Sourcebook of Sacred Texts.* Philadelphia: University of Pennsylvania Press, 1987.

Milbank, John. *The Word Made Strange: Theology, Language, Culture.* Oxford: Blackwell Publishers, 1997.

Milgrom, Jacob. *Leviticus 17–22: A New Translation with Introduction and Commentary.* Anchor Bible, vol 3A. New York: Doubleday, 1991.

Millar, William R. *Priesthood in Ancient Israel.* St. Louis, MO: Chalice Press, 2001.

Miller, John W. *How the Bible Came to Be: Exploring the Narrative and Message.* New York: Paulist Press, 2004.

Miller, John W. *The Origins of the Bible: Rethinking Canon History.* New York: Paulist Press, 1994.

Milner, Paulinus, O.P., ed. *The Ministry of the Word.* Collegeville, MN: Liturgical Press, 1967.

Minear, Paul S. *Horizons of Christian Community.* St. Louis: Bethany Press, 1959.

Moran, Gabriel, F.S.C. *Scripture and Tradition: A Survey of the Controversy.* New York: Herder and Herder, 1963.

Mork, Dom Wulstan, O.S.B. *Transformed by Grace: Scripture, Sacraments and the Sonship of Christ.* Cincinnati, OH: Servant Books, 2004.

Morrison, Karl F. *"I AM YOU": The Hermeneutics of Empathy in Western Literature, Theology, and Art.* Princeton, NJ: Princeton University Press, 1988.

Murphy-O'Connor, Jerome. *St. Paul's Corinth.* Wilmington, DE: Michael Glazier, 1983.

Murray, Robert, S.J. *The Cosmic Covenant: Biblical Themes of Justice, Peace, and the Integrity of Creation.* London: Sheed and Ward, 1992.

Naduvilezham, Joseph. *The Theology of the Paschal Lamb in Ephrem of Nisibis.* Kerala, India: Oriental Institute of Religious Studies India, 2000.

Nassif, Bradley, ed. *New Perspectives on Historical Theology: Essays in Memory of John Meyendorff.* Grand Rapids, MI: Eerdmans, 1996.

Neuhaus, Richard John, ed. *Biblical Interpretation in Crisis: The Ratzinger Conference on Bible and Church.* Grand Rapids, MI: Eerdmans, 1989.

Neusner, Jacob. *Making God's Word Work: A Guide to the Mishnah.* New York: Continuum, 2004.

Newman, John Henry Cardinal. *An Essay on the Development of Christian Doctrine.* New York: Doubleday, 1960.

Nicoll, W. Robertson. *The Expositor's Greek Testament.* 4 vols. London: Hodder and Stoughton, 1912.

Niditch, Susan. *Oral World and Written Word: Ancient Israelite Literature.* Louisville, KY: Westminster John Knox Press, 1996.

Nielsen, J. T. *Adam and Christ in the Theology of Irenaeus of Lyons.* Gronigen: Van Gorcum, 1968.

Ninow, F. *Indicators of Typology Within the Old Testament: The Exodus Motif.* New York: Peter Lang, 2001.

Ocker, Christopher. *Biblical Poetics Before Humanism and Reformation.* Cambridge: Cambridge University Press, 2002.

O'Connor, Rev. James T. *Land of the Living: A Theology of the Last Things.* New York: Catholic Book Publishing, 1992.

Old, Hughes Oliphant. *The Reading and Preaching of the Scriptures in the Worship of the Christian Church.* 3 vols. Grand Rapids, MI: Eerdmans, 1998–1999.

———. *Themes and Variations for a Christian Doxology: Some Thoughts on the Theology of Worship.* Grand Rapids, MI: Eerdmans, 1992.

Olsen, Glenn W. *Beginning at Jerusalem: Five Reflections on the History of the Church.* San Francisco: Ignatius Press, 2004.

O'Neill, Colman E., O.P. *Meeting Christ in the Sacraments.* New York: Alba House, 1964.

———. *Sacramental Realism: A General Theory of Sacraments.* Wilmington, DE: Michael Glazier, 1983.

Ong, Walter J., S.J. *Orality and Literacy: The Technologizing of the Word.* New York: Routledge, 1982.

———. *The Presence of the Word: Some Prolegomena for Cultural and Religious History.* New Haven, CT: Yale University Press, 1967.

Osborn, Eric. *Irenaeus of Lyons.* Cambridge: Cambridge University Press, 2001.

Ostborn, Gunnar. *Cult and Canon: A Study in the Canonization of the Old Testament.* Uppsala: A.-B. Lundequistska Bokhandeln, 1950.

Parry, Donald W., ed. *Temples of the Ancient World: Ritual and Symbolism.* Salt Lake City: Deseret Book Company, 1994.

Parry, Donald W., and Stephen D. Ricks, eds. *The Temple in Time and Eternity.* Provo, UT: Brigham Young University, 1999.

Pattemore, Stephen. *The People of God in the Apocalypse: Discourse, Structure and Exegesis.* Cambridge: Cambridge University Press, 2004.

Paulinus of Nola. *The Poems of St. Paulinus of Nola.* New York: Newman Press, 1975.

Pelikan, Jaroslav. *Christianity and Classical Culture: The Metamorphosis of Natural Theology in the Christian Encounter with Hellenism.* New Haven, CT: Yale University Press, 1993.

———. *The Emergence of the Catholic Tradition (100–600).* Chicago: University of Chicago Press, 1971.

———. *Interpreting the Bible and the Constitution.* New Haven, CT: Yale University Press, 2004.

———. *The Mystery of Continuity: Time and History, Memory and Eternity in the Thought of Saint Augustine.* Charlottesville, VA: University of Virginia Press, 1986.

———. *Whose Bible Is It? A History of the Scriptures Through the Ages.* New York: Viking, 2005.

Peterson, Erik. *The Angels and the Liturgy.* New York: Herder and Herder, 1964.

Philo. *Works of Philo.* Peabody, MA: Hendrickson, 1993.

Pickstock, Catherine. *After Writing: On the Liturgical Consummation of Philosophy.* Oxford: Blackwell Publishers, 1998.

Pitkanen, Pekka. *Central Sanctuary and Centralization of Worship in Ancient Israel: From the Settlement to the Building of Solomon's Temple.* Piscataway, NJ: Gorgias Press, 2003.

Plescia, J. *The Oath and Perjury in Ancient Greece.* Tallahassee: Florida State University Press, 1970.

Poorthuis, M., and J. Schwartz. *Purity and Holiness: The Heritage of Leviticus.* Leiden: Brill, 2000.

Poovathanikunnel, Thomas. *The Sacraments: The Mystery Revealed.* Kerala, India: Oriental Institute of Religious Studies India, 1998.

Power, David Noel. *"The Word of the Lord": Liturgy's Use of Scripture.* Maryknoll, NY: Orbis, 2001.

Powery, Emerson B. *Jesus Reads Scripture: The Function of Jesus' Use of Scripture in the Synoptic Gospels.* Leiden: Brill, 2003.

Pseudo-Dionysius the Areopagite. *Pseudo-Dionysius: The Complete Works.* New York: Paulist Press, 1987.

Quasten, Johannes, ed. *Patrology.* 4 vols. Allen, TX: Christian Classics, no date.

Radner, Ephraim, and George Sumner, eds. *The Rule of Faith: Scripture, Canon, and Creed in a Critical Age.* Harrisburg, PA: Morehouse Publishing, 1998.

Rahner, Hugo, S.J. *A Theology of Proclamation.* New York: Herder and Herder, 1968.

Rahner, Karl, and Joseph Ratzinger. *Revelation and Tradition.* New York: Herder and Herder, 1966.

Ratzinger, Joseph Cardinal. *Church, Ecumenism and Politics.* New York: Crossroad, 1988.

———. *Eschatology.* Washington, DC: Catholic University of America Press, 1988.

———. *Feast of Faith.* San Francisco: Ignatius Press, 1986.

———. *Many Religions—One Covenant: Israel, the Church, and the World.* San Francisco: Ignatius Press, 1999.

———. *The Meaning of Christian Brotherhood.* San Francisco: Ignatius Press, 1995.

———. *The Nature and Mission of Theology: Approaches to Understanding Its Role in the Light of Present Controversy.* San Francisco: Ignatius Press, 1995.

———. *The Spirit of the Liturgy.* San Francisco: Ignatius Press, 2000.

———. *A New Song for the Lord: Faith in Christ and Liturgy Today.* New York: Crossroad, 1997.

Regan, David. *Experience the Mystery: Pastoral Possibilities for Christian Mystagogy.* London: Geoffrey Chapman, 1994.

Reid, Alcuin, O.S.B. *The Organic Development of the Liturgy: The Principles of Liturgical Reform and Their Relation to the Twentieth Century Liturgical Movement Prior to the Second Vatican Council.* Farnsborough, England: Saint Michael's Abbey Press, 2004.

Riley, William. *King and Cultus in Chronicles: Worship and the Reinterpretation of History.* Sheffield: Sheffield Academic Press, 1993.

Robinson, John A. T. *Redating the New Testament.* Philadelphia: Fortress Press, 1976.

Rose, Sr. Sophy, C.M.C. *Church as Mystery and Communion.* Kerala, India: Oriental Institute of Religious Studies India, 1998.

Rowell, Geoffrey, ed. *Tradition Renewed: The Oxford Movement Conference Papers.* Allison Park, PA: Pickwick Publications, 1986.

Rutledge, Dom Denys. *Cosmic Theology: The Ecclesiastical Hierarchy of Pseudo-Denys: An Introduction.* London: Routledge and Kegan Paul, 1964.

Sanders, Fred. *The Image of the Immanent Trinity: Rahner's Rule and the Theological Interpretation of Scripture.* New York: Peter Lang, 2005.

Sanders, James A. *From Sacred Story to Sacred Text.* Philadelphia: Fortress Press, 1987.

Sarapion of Thmuis. *Bishop Sarapion's Prayer-Book*. London: SPCK, 1899.

Sarna, Nahum. *Exploring Exodus: The Heritage of Biblical Israel*. New York: Schocken, 1986.

———. *Understanding Genesis: The Heritage of Biblical Israel*. New York: Random House, 1988.

Satterlee, Craig Alan. *Ambrose of Milan's Method of Mystagogical Preaching*. Collegeville, MN: Liturgical Press, 2002.

Sauter, Gerhard, and John Barton, eds. *Revelation and Story: Narrative Theology and the Centrality of Story*. Burlington, VT: Ashgate, 2000.

Scalise, Charles J. *From Scripture to Theology: A Canonical Journey into Hermeneutics*. Downers Grove, IL: InterVarsity Press, 1996.

Schaefer, Francis J. "The Tabernacle: Its History, Structure and Custody," *The Ecclesiastical Review* 92, no. 4 (1935): 449–68.

Scheeben, Matthias J. *The Mysteries of Christianity*. St. Louis: Herder, 1950.

Schelkle, Karl Hermann. "Sacred Scripture and Word of God." In *Dogmatic vs. Biblical Theology*. Edited by Herbert Vorgrimler. London: Burns and Oates, 1964.

Schloen, J. David. *The House of the Father as Fact and Symbol: Patrimonialism in Ugarit and the Ancient Near East*. Winona Lake, IN: Eisenbrauns, 2001.

Schmaus, Michael. *Preaching as a Saving Encounter*. Staten Island, NY: Alba House, 1966.

Schmemann, Alexander. *For the Life of the World*. New York: St. Vladimir's Seminary Press, 1973.

———. *Introduction to Liturgical Theology*. Bangor, ME: The Faith Press, 1966.

———. *The Eucharist*. Crestwood, NY: St. Vladimir's Seminary Press, 1988.

Schniedewind, William M. *How the Bible Became a Book*. Cambridge: Cambridge University Press, 2004.

Schweiker, William. *Mimetic Reflections: A Study in Hermeneutics, Theology, and Ethics*. New York: Fordham University Press, 1990.

Segal, Alan. *Rebecca's Children: Judaism and Christianity in the Roman World*. Cambridge, MA: Harvard University Press, 1986.

Seitz, C. R. *Figured Out: Typology and Providence in Christian Scripture.* Louisville, KY: Westminster John Knox Press, 2001.

Selzer, Eugene P. *Rupert of Deutz: Preaching the Word of God.* Rome: Pontificium Athenaeum Anselmianum, 1968.

Senn, Frank. "The Bible and the Liturgy," in *Liturgy* 19, no. 3 (2004): 5ff.

Shands, Alfred. *The Liturgical Movement and the Local Church.* New York: Morehouse-Barlow Co., 1966.

Shepherd, Massey H., Jr. *The Paschal Liturgy and the Apocalypse.* Edited by J. G. Davies and A. Raymond George. London: Lutterworth Press, 1960.

————, ed. *Worship in Scripture and Tradition.* New York: Oxford University Press, 1963.

————. *The Worship of the Church.* Greenwich, CT: Seabury Press, 1952.

Shriver, George H. *Contemporary Reflections on the Medieval Christian Tradition: Essays in Honor of Ray C. Petry.* Durham, NC: Duke University Press, 1974.

Simon, Ulrich. *The Ascent to Heaven.* London: Barrie and Rockliff, 1958.

————. *Heaven in the Christian Tradition.* New York: Harper & Brothers, 1958.

Simonetti, Manlio. *Biblical Interpretation in the Early Church.* Edinburgh: T. & T. Clark, 1994.

Skarsaune, Oskar. *In the Shadow of the Temple: Jewish Influences on Early Christianity.* Downers Grove, IL: InterVarsity Press, 2002.

Sloyan, Gerard. "The Liturgical Proclamation of the Word of God." In *Bible, Life, and Worship: Twenty-Second North American Liturgical Week.* Washington, DC: The Liturgical Conference, 1961.

Smemmelroth, Otto, S.J. *The Preaching Word: On the Theology of Proclamation.* New York: Herder and Herder, 1965.

Smith, Mark S., with contributions by Elizabeth M. Bloch-Smith. *The Pilgrimage Pattern in Exodus.* Sheffield: Sheffield Academic Press, 1997.

Socias, James, ed. *Reflections on the Catechism of the Catholic Church.* Chicago: Midwest Theological Forum, 1993.

Sokolowski, Robert. *Eucharistic Presence: A Study in the Theology of Dis-*

closure. Washington, DC: The Catholic University of America Press, 1993.

Spatofora, A. *From the "Temple of God" to God as the Temple: A Biblical Theological Study of the Temple in the Book of Revelation.* Rome: Gregorian University Press, 1997.

Spidlík, Thomas. *Drinking from the Hidden Fountain: A Patristic Breviary.* Kalamazoo, MI: Cistercian Publications, 1994.

Steinmann, Andrew E. *The Oracles of God: The Old Testament Canon.* Saint Louis: Concordia Academic Press, 1999.

Stewart, James S. *A Faith to Proclaim: The Content of Effective Preaching.* New York: Charles Scribner's Sons, 1953.

Strasbourg Congress. *The Liturgy and the Word of God.* Collegeville, MN: Liturgical Press, 1959.

Stravinskas, Peter. *The Bible and the Mass.* Mount Pocono, PA: Newman House Press, 2000.

Stuhlmueller, Carroll, C.P. *Thirsting for the Lord: Essays in Biblical Spirituality.* Staten Island, NY: Alba House, 1977.

Stuhlmueller, Carroll, and Sebaastian MacDonald, eds. *A Voice Crying Out in the Desert: Preparing for Vatican II with Barnabas M. Ahern.* Collegeville, MN: Liturgical Press, 1996.

Sundberg, Albert C., Jr. *The Old Testament of the Early Church.* Cambridge, MA: Harvard University Press, 1964.

Swanston, Hamish F.G. *The Community Witness: An Exploration of Some of the Influences at Work in the New Testament Community and Its Writings.* New York: Sheed and Ward, 1967.

Taft, Robert F., S.J. *Beyond East and West: Problems in Liturgical Understanding.* 2nd ed. Rome: Pontifical Oriental Institute, 1997.

Tambiah, S.J. *A Performative Approach to Ritual.* Oxford: Oxford University Press, 1981.

Taylor, Michael J. *Liturgical Renewal in the Christian Churches.* Baltimore: Helicon Press Inc., 1967.

Theodore of Mopsuestia. *Commentary on the Twelve Prophets.* Washington, DC: Catholic University of America Press, 2004.

Thiselton, Anthony C. *The Two Horizons: New Testament Hermeneutics and Philosophical Description.* Grand Rapids, MI: Eerdmans, 1980.

Thompson, Claude H. *Theology of the Kerygma: A Study in Primitive Preaching.* Englewood Cliffs, NJ: Prentice-Hall, 1962.

Thompson, Leonard L. *The Book of Revelation: Apocalypse and Empire.* New York: Oxford University Press, 1990.

Thompson, William M. *The Struggle for Theology's Soul: Contesting Scripture in Christology.* New York: Crossroad, 1996.

Thurian, Max. *The Eucharistic Memorial.* Richmond, VA: John Knox Press, 1962.

———. *Visible Unity and Tradition.* London: Darton, Longman, and Todd, 1964.

Tkacz, Catherine Brown. *The Key to the Brescia Casket: Typology and the Early Christian Imagination.* Notre Dame, IN: University of Notre Dame Press, 2002.

Tomson, P. J. "The New Testament Canon as the Embodiment of Evolving Christian Attitudes Towards the Jews." In *Canonization and Decanonization.* Edited by A. Van Der Kooij and K. Van Der Toorn. Leiden: Brill, 1998.

Trocmé, Etienne. *The Passion as Liturgy.* London: SCM Press, 1983.

Tournay, R. J. *Seeing and Hearing God with the Psalms: The Prophetic Liturgy of the Second Temple in Jerusalem.* Sheffield: Sheffield Academic Press, 1991.

Tucker, G. M., and D. Knight, eds. *Humanizing America's Iconic Book.* Chico, CA: Scholars Press, 1982.

Turner, Harold W. *From Temple to Meeting House: The Phenomenology and Theology of Places of Worship.* New York: Mouton Publishers, 1979.

Vagaggini, Dom Cyprian, O.S.B. *Theological Dimensions of the Liturgy.* Collegeville, MN: Liturgical Press, 1976.

VanderKam, James C. *From Revelation and Canon.* Leiden: Brill, 2000.

van der Kooij, A., and K. van der Toorn. *Canonization and Decanonization: Papers Presented to the International Conference of the Leiden Institute for the Study of Religions (Lisor), Held at Leiden 9–10 January 1997.* Leiden: Brill, 1998.

van Henten, Jan Willem, and Anton Houtepen, eds. *Religious Identity and the Invention of Tradition: Papers Read at a NOSTER Conference in Soesterberg, January 4–6, 1999.*

Vanhoye, Albert, S.J. *Old Testament Priests and New Priests According to the New Testament.* Petersham, MA: St. Bede's Publications, 1986.

Van Olst, E. H. *The Bible and Liturgy.* Grand Rapids, MI: Eerdmans, 1991.

Vansina, Jan. *Oral Tradition as History.* Madison: University of Wisconsin Press, 1985.

Varghese, Baby. *West Syrian Liturgical Theology.* Burlington, VT: Ashgate, 2004.

Vasholz, Robert. *The Old Testament Canon in the Old Testament Church: The Internal Rationale for Old Testament Canonicity.* Ceredigion, United Kingdom: The Edwin Mellen Press, Ltd., 1990.

Velamparampil, Dr. Cyrus. *The Celebration of the Liturgy of the Word in the Syro-Malabar Qurbana: A Biblico-Theological Analysis.* Kerala, India: Oriental Institute of Religious Studies India Publications, 1997.

Verheul, A. *Introduction to the Liturgy: Towards a Theology of Worship.* Collegeville, MN: Liturgical Press, 1968.

Viagulamuthu, Xavier Paul B. *Offering Our Bodies as a Living Sacrifice to God: A Study in Pauline Spirituality Based on Romans 12,1.* Rome: Editrice Pontificia Universita Gregoriana, 2002.

Vogel, Dwight W., ed. *Primary Sources of Liturgical Theology: A Reader.* Collegeville, MN: Liturgical Press, 2000.

Vonier, Dom Anscar, O.S.B. *The New and Eternal Covenant.* New York: Benziger Brothers, 1930.

Von Rad, Gerhard. *Wisdom in Israel.* London: SCM, 1993.

Wainwright, Geoffrey. *Doxology: The Praise of God in Worship, Doctrine, and Life.* New York: Oxford University Press, 1980.

Wainwright, Geoffrey. *Eucharist and Eschatology.* New York: Oxford University Press, 1981.

Wainwright, Geoffrey. *Worship with One Accord: Where Liturgy and Ecumenism Embrace.* New York: Oxford University Press, 1997.

Wakefield, Gordon S. *The Liturgy of St. John.* London: Epworth, 1985.

Wannenwetsch, Bernd. *Political Worship: Ethics for Christian Citizens.* New York: Oxford University Press, 2004.

Wansbrough, Henry, ed. *Jesus and the Oral Tradition.* Sheffield: JSOT Press, 1991.

Watson, Francis. *Text and Truth*. Grand Rapids, MI: Eerdmans, 1997.

Watson, Francis. *Text, Church, and World: Biblical Interpretation in Theological Perspective*. Grand Rapids, MI: Eerdmans, 1994.

Webb, Stephen H. *The Divine Voice: Christian Proclamation and the Theology of Sound*. Grand Rapids, MI: Brazos Press, 2004.

Webber, Robert E., ed. *The Biblical Foundations of Christian Worship*. Nashville, TN: Star Song Publishing Group, 1993.

Wenham, Gordon J. *Numbers: An Introduction and Commentary*. Downers Grove, IL: InterVarsity Press, 1981.

Werner, Eric. *The Sacred Bridge*. New York: Columbia University Press, 1959.

West, Fritz. *Scripture and Memory: The Ecumenical Hermeneutic of the Three-Year Lectionaries*. Collegeville, MN: Liturgical Press, 1997.

Westcott, Brooke Foss. *A General Survey of History of the Canon of the New Testament*. 6th ed. Grand Rapids, MI: Baker Book House, 1980.

Westermann, Claus, ed. *Essays on Old Testament Hermeneutics*. Richmond, VA: John Knox Press, 1964.

Wiebe, Phillip H. *God and Other Spirits: Intimations of Transcendence in Christian Experience*. Oxford: Oxford University Press, 2004.

Wilder, Terry L. *Pseudonymity, the New Testament, and Deception: An Inquiry into Intention and Reception*. Lanham, MD: University Press of America, 2004.

Wilken, Robert L. "Angels and Archangels: The Worship of Heaven and Earth," in *Antiphon* 6, no. 1 (2001).

———. *Judaism and the Early Christian Mind: A Study of Cyril of Alexandria's Exegesis and Theology*. New Haven, CT: Yale University Press, 1971.

———. *Remembering the Christian Past*. Grand Rapids, MI: Eerdmans, 1995.

———. *The Spirit of Early Christian Thought: Seeking the Face of God*. New Haven, CT: Yale University Press, 2003.

Wilkinson, John. *From Synagogue to Church: The Traditional Design*. New York: RoutledgeCurzon, 2002.

———. *Interpretation and Community*. London: Macmillan, 1963.

Witvliet, John D. *Worship Seeking Understanding: Windows into Christian Practice.* Grand Rapids, MI: Baker Academic, 2003.

Work, Telford. *Living and Active: Scripture in the Economy of Salvation.* Grand Rapids, MI: Eerdmans, 2002.

Wright, Christopher J. H. *Knowing Jesus Through the Old Testament.* Downers Grove, IL: InterVarsity Press, 1992.

Wright, N. T. The *New Testament and the People of God.* Minneapolis, MN: Fortress Press, 1992.

Wyatt, Nicolas. *Space and Time in the Religious Life of the Near East.* Sheffield: Sheffield Academic Press, 2001.

Yarnold, Edward, S.J. *The Awe-Inspiring Rites of Initiation.* Collegeville, MN: Liturgical Press, 1994.

Young, Frances M. *Biblical Exegesis and the Formation of Christian Culture.* Peabody, MA: Hendrickson, 2002.

Young, Frances M. *The Use of Sacrificial Ideas in Greek Christian Writers from the New Testament to John Chrysostom.* Cambridge, MA: The Philadelphia Patristic Foundation, 1979.

Young, Robin Darling. *In Procession Before the World: Martyrdom as Public Liturgy in Early Christianity.* Milwaukee, WI: Marquette University Press, 2001.

INDEX

INDEX

INDEX

INDEX

Sacraments, 28, 180n21
Sacramentum, 66–68
Sacrifices, 57
Sacrosanctum Concilium, 120
Sainthood, 171
Sanders, James A., 35
Scanlin, Harold P., 183n25
Scheeben, M. J., 5
Schmemann, Alexander, 96, 99
Schonborn, Cardinal Christoph,
    18–19, 27, 193n21
"Scientific" study of scripture, 162,
    167
Scripture
  communion and, 167–72
  interpretation of, 137–39,
      163–67
  sacramentality of, 81–86, 186n6,
      187n14
  "senses" of, 166
Scripture-liturgy relationship, 12
  formal relationship, 34–35,
      46–52
  intrinsic liturgicality of scripture,
      35–36
  material relationship, 34, 36–46
  See also Covenant; Liturgical
      proclamation; *Parousia;*
      Remembrance; Tradition
Second Vatican Council, 3, 82–83,
    120, 125–26. *See also Dei
    Verbum*
Segal, Alan, 68, 69, 95, 111
Serapion, bishop of Antioch,
    51–52
"Seven," etymology of Hebrew
    word for, 60–61
Sifre Deuteronomy, 60
Sloyan, Gerard, 47
Sola scriptura, 142

Solomon, 41, 55, 64, 112
Sommer, Benjamin D., 182n23,
    194n1
Spiritual sense of scripture, 166
Stephen, 104–5, 108, 111
Stuhlmueller, Carroll, 46–47,
    173
Summa Theologica (Thomas Aquinas),
    165

Taft, Robert, 25–26
Tatian, 83
Ten Commandments, 39–40, 63
Tertullian, 67, 133, 137
Theodore of Mopsuestia, 30, 76,
    161–62
Theodosius, emperor, 190n23
Theologia, 17–18
Theophany, 168–70, 171
Theophilus, 83
Theopneustos, 78–79
Thomas Aquinas, 23, 165
Thompson, Leonard, 151
Thurian, Max, 91, 92, 93, 98,
    137
Todah, 65–66
Tomson, P. J., 48–49
Tradition, xv, 124–42
  authority in the church and,
      138–42, 196n29
  covenant and, 130–31
  interpreting scripture and,
      137–39
  in Judaism, 124–25
  lectionary and, 135–37
  "living tradition" concept,
      125–26, 128–29, 131–34
  Pauline perspective on, 126–28

237